THE INTERLOPER

The Interloper

LESSONS FROM RESISTANCE IN THE FIELD

Michel Anteby

PRINCETON UNIVERSITY PRESS

PRINCETON & OXFORD

Requests for permission to reproduce material from this work should be sent to permissions@press.princeton.edu

Published by Princeton University Press
41 William Street, Princeton, New Jersey 08540
99 Banbury Road, Oxford OX2 6JX

press.princeton.edu

ISBN: 9780691255361
ISBN (pbk.): 9780691255378
ISBN (e-book): 9780691255415

British Library Cataloging-in-Publication Data is available

Editorial: Meagan Levinson & Erik Beranek
Production Editorial: Jaden Young
Jacket/Cover Design: Heather Hansen
Production: Erin Suydam
Publicity: William Pagdatoon

This book has been composed in Arno

10 9 8 7 6 5 4 3 2 1

In memory of my father, aunt, and uncle,
who all taught me about resistance in their own ways.

CONTENTS

THE INTERLOPER

Introduction

"CATCH," HE CALLED OUT LOUDLY. I was in the rather dark office of the director of the Maryland State Anatomy Board. I couldn't fully distinguish what he had thrown at me. From afar, it seemed the size of a baseball and soft to the touch. Regardless, I wanted to be a good sport. After all, I was an outsider trying to get the director to agree to let me enter—and study—his professional world. He oversaw the handling of human cadavers donated to his program for medical education and research. I caught the object awkwardly but nonetheless managed not to drop it. He smiled and told me I was now holding in my hands a bull's plastinated testicle.

It was in that moment that I finally felt I had paid my dues and should be granted access. I can only guess that he was trying to test my commitment to the field.[1] I also knew this director was my last chance of entering the world of whole-body donation. This business of securing cadavers intrigued me as a field researcher because of its moral ambiguity. But by then, and after a year of attempting to study US donation programs, so many doors had been slammed that I was starting to consider changing research topics. People all over the country had politely declined my request to even begin a conversation on the possibility of conducting research with them.

So, I was nervous, and for a good reason. This director was my only remaining contact who had not yet officially turned me down. I had flown to Baltimore to meet him. The visit included a memorable drive in his convertible across the Chesapeake Bay, where he quizzed me on my motives and more. I felt good about my handling of his questions. The clear sky and shining sun made for a promising occasion. Alas, no access materialized during the drive. Nor did he commit to access after I caught, with relief, the well-preserved testicle. Instead, he went on to explain his technique of using liquid polymer to replace water and fat in body parts and even bodies.

The catch felt like the culmination of a series of tests he had put me through. Despite succeeding at all of them, I still could not predict whether he would say "yes." When the phone call came a few days later inviting me to study his archives of donations, I felt elated. I remember clearly the bliss and excitement of finally obtaining a green light to enter the field.[2] As I hung up the phone, I started planning my next trip to Baltimore. The waiting was over. At last, my journey, it seemed, had finally begun.

Most field researchers can recount the exact moment when the mythical door finally opened for them. And several report a sense of bliss and relief, much like my own, after being granted access to a field. When the anthropologist Paul Rabinow, for instance, embarked on his fieldwork researching the tribal area surrounding a walled market town in Morocco, access was not a given. It took him months to finally settle in the nearby village, which only then was he able to begin studying. Along the way, a flurry of encounters, missed connections, and wrong turns hindered his access, as he strikingly recalls in *Reflections on Fieldwork in Morocco* (1977). But halfway through his account, a break occurred: "Finally, word came from the village: I could move in," he reported. "The next week was joyously spent in making preparations, buying provisions, and feeling relieved. So what if my Arabic was weak and I was entering a hostile situation; the 'real' fieldwork was finally under way."[3]

These experiences are far from unique and in fact are shared by many field researchers. Whether "the fate" of a project lies in a gatekeeper's hands[4] or in alternating for months between a "foot in the door" and "door in the face" strategy to find access,[5] the sudden relief is immense. Tellingly, many articles, book sections, and even entire books are devoted to this precise topic within the general subject of accessing a field. Titles such as *Gaining Access: A Practical and Theoretical Guide for Qualitative Researchers*[6] and "The Social Psychology of Access in Ethnographic Research"[7] point to the anxiety associated with each failed attempt.[8] Unsurprisingly, and as the sociologist Diane Vaughan concludes, "getting access to a research setting is often described in text-books as a glorious moment when the gates open and you are in."[9]

Perhaps this is why it might seem, as Rabinow's above use of quotation marks suggests, that the "real" fieldwork starts only once access is gained. But that is far from the case. In fact—as this book will demonstrate—all the time spent prior to gaining access is *also* fieldwork. Moreover, even once "in" the field, all attempts by others to *prevent* researchers from conducting their inquiries remain part of fieldwork. For most field researchers, the boundary between being in and out is never really settled.[10] Gaining and maintaining access is therefore a dynamic process that's best envisioned as continuously walking down "a hallway with many doors," rather than simply opening the proverbial single door.[11]

Importantly, as we go down these hallways and attempt to open doors, we inevitably stop being simply outsiders and become something else: "interlopers." By interlopers, I mean individuals who intrude into places, situations, or activities and disrupt the status quo by examining other people's affairs, even when trying to blend in. Fieldworkers are typical of the figure of the interloper; but any change agent, such as a labor organizer or advocate for an issue using a social movement's parlance, is also an interloper.[12] Consequently, other field participants commonly engage in elaborate resistance efforts to push interlopers back.

I know this firsthand, since I have gone down many of these intricate hallways in search of an elusive access and have encountered such pushback. These are forms of *resistance*—or the social mechanisms deployed by groups (such as organizations, professions, families, etc.) to maintain the status quo—and it is with such resistance that this book is concerned. Here, I argue that the forms of resistance that interlopers face are much more telling than usually acknowledged. All this pushback might seemingly be discounted as "non-knowledge," yet it constitutes very rich data.[13] Put simply, such resistance offers a mostly overlooked yet powerful lens to grasp social worlds.

To illuminate these dynamics, *The Interloper* brings together stories and insights from several instances of resistance that I encountered or witnessed when entering or progressing in a field. The book analyzes, for instance, what happens when an ethnographer is voted out of a meeting of clinical anatomists intent on maintaining their professional jurisdiction, or when a doctoral candidate appears at the gates of a French factory that refuses to acknowledge its Nazi past. The book also examines what occurs when labor organizers try to unionize Disneyland puppeteers, as management aims for the show to go on. (I will explain later the traction gained by including this seemingly distinct case.) In addition, the book explores what transpires when a junior researcher gets stalked by Transportation Security Administration (TSA) staff while trying to observe their operations; a newly hired Harvard Business School (HBS) professor gets silenced for asking the wrong questions; and ghostwriters deny they are ghostwriters in interviews despite clear evidence suggesting otherwise. Across all these diverse contexts, I show how fieldworkers can benefit from resistance.

Many field researchers, regardless of how they enter, end up becoming interlopers and eventually face the resistance detailed in this book. Despite their aspirations to blend in and their hopes of being considered insiders, they embark on a very different trajectory than those they talk to, observe, often joke with, and get to know. Even in settings where they are initially invited into a field[14] or were field participants themselves before they started their study,[15] I suspect that the person's invited or insider status rapidly morphs into something more nebulous and occasionally even more threatening.[16] And that means that many researchers need to deal to some extent with resistance to interlopers, like themselves, in the field.[17]

My own awareness of the hurdles thrown up before field researchers was undoubtedly heightened by my research interests in morally tainted topics and secretive settings. Over the years, my studies have included factory workers producing illegal artifacts with company materials and time, ghostwriters drafting the memoirs of those they refer to somewhat cheekily as the "talent" (i.e., the person *not* writing), and of course, clinical anatomists trying to secure human cadavers for their medical schools. None of these topics were easy to pursue. Also, several of the organizations I examined—TSA, Disneyland, and HBS—were quite secretive about the conduct of their work.[18]

In most instances, fieldworkers do not think twice about these obstacles and simply continue attempting to find alternate ways to do their work.[19] They carry, at best, a vague imprint of these bumps along the way and occasionally remember them when similar interactions or situations occur. In some cases, the bump is suddenly made visible and becomes quite salient. At one point, even after settling into his field, Rabinow found a delegation of villagers at his door informing him that they could no longer work with him because they suspected that the government did not approve of his pursuit. Until the issue was resolved, no one would talk to him.[20] Yet such stumbling blocks are not always so clear. Instead, in most fields and organizations, reactions to interlopers' tentative intrusions are less overt.

Covert forms of resistance are more common, I suspect, than overt ones or open disagreements in many contexts. In the corporate world in particular, conflicts rarely "escalate into large-scale public disputes or firings."[21] In such settings, even in the exact venues that are meant for the purpose of surfacing potential disagreements (such as review or project advancement meetings), as one participant aptly remarks, "No one wants to say no. We're not good at killing things."[22] The angry group of opponents barging into an office to confront an interloper and the vibrant shouting matches epitomized in heroic corporate sagas are probably outliers. Likewise, few field interlopers can point to a formal and precise trace of a refusal.

Oftentimes, researchers encounter subtle and repeated pushback from field participants, which is more than just annoying. Indeed, on closer inspection, some behaviors can be seen for what they really are: namely, covert forms of field resistance. Consider the third time a potential informant fails to reply to your outreach attempt on a given topic. An act—or lack of action—that might initially be coded as anecdotal and due to overwork can suddenly take on a new meaning.[23] Also, consider the way an interviewee might systematically forget certain past events (e.g., a contested merger) yet perfectly recall other contemporaneous ones (e.g., a new product launch). Again, what might initially appear to be random acts of forgetfulness slowly coalesce into a pattern harder to ignore. All these and other similar behaviors constitute forms of covert field resistance, which permeate a fieldworker's journey.[24]

By covert resistance, I mean the ways in which a field resists in non-overt ways attempts by interlopers (most notably field researchers) to inquire about its inner workings. This book discusses these forms of defense or resistance and asks what they can tell us about the given fields that harbor them.[25] I will use the terms *resistance* and *defense* interchangeably as they constitute two facets of the same phenomenon. From interlopers' viewpoint, the phenomenon codes as a form of resistance to their inquiries. From participants', it is seen as a form of defense against an outside inquiry.[26]

Left in a general form, the occurrence of covert resistance might seem like a juicy conversation topic for water-cooler meetings, after-work drink outings, and private exchanges. However, if we collect and analyze more systematically such occurrences across settings, countries, and even time periods, we can transform the puzzling existence of this resistance into a problem for a broader inquiry that allows us to answer some important questions. For example, what are typical forms of covert field resistance, and how can we increase our awareness of their existence? In addition, why are certain forms found in some fields but not in others? Crucially, what can these forms teach us about these fields? Finally, how might we—as interlopers—be impacted by the repeated experience of specific forms of resistance, and what might they say about us?

These are only some of the questions covered in this book. *The Interloper* is not an exhaustive review of all resistance behaviors. Instead, it builds on several in-depth cases and offers a framework to better understand typical forms of covert field resistance. Moreover, the book also invites field researchers to search for empirically grounded explanations for these and other instances of resistance. I chose to focus on covert forms of resistance because they tend to be easier to miss, but the framework could be extended to overt forms as well.[27]

The framework presented here anchors forms of covert field resistance in the explanatory power and analytical possibilities that they offer in a given field. It also examines the implications for interlopers in confronting select forms of resistance. Furthermore, the analysis presents six main types of covert field resistance: "obstructing," "hiding," "shelving," "silencing," "forgetting," and "denying."[28] *Obstructing* is examined in the context of whole-body donations (chapter 1), *hiding* at the TSA (chapter 2), *shelving* at Disneyland (chapter 3), *silencing* at HBS (chapter 4), *forgetting* in a French aeronautics factory (chapter 5), and *denying* among ghostwriters (chapter 6). Together, these forms of resistance can be combined to make a field researcher's inquiry unsuccessful, or so it may seem.

I write about these six types because I suspect that they are the most common ones. That said, I can imagine many more resistance or defense mechanisms. As illustrations, interlopers can also be suddenly deemed no longer legally "compliant" with an institutional requirement, put under intensive daily surveillance, or even sexually harassed in the field.[29] Such forms of resistance, though less common, are probably much more troubling from an interloper's perspective.

So, how does field resistance work? And how does its functioning inform us as researchers? There are two main answers, which permeate the whole book.

First, when navigating fields, our simple presence can trigger defense mechanisms.[30] These dynamics can happen whether we want them to or not. This "field reactivity" is integral to our endeavors.[31] For example, a mere expressed interest in a topic or the most benign question can quickly lead others to cast us in an interloper role, even without our knowledge. Those of us a bit less polished in our self-presentation (and I include myself among them) might more frequently trigger such typecasting and a range of possible associated defensive reactions among field participants.

Unsurprisingly, key gatekeepers in any field are often reluctant to have an interloper tell their story.[32] They prefer circulating a more practiced narrative that they can control—one that usually best reflects on them. This baseline resistance to the dissemination of competing stories is a way for them to patrol the varied ecology of storytelling that directly shapes their lives.[33] Frequently, however, the pushback does not end there. Above and beyond it, layers of field-specific cultural understandings can inform field participants' (including gatekeepers') reactions to interlopers.

Many such forms of added resistance are retrospectively useful.[34] As the sociologist Japonica Brown-Saracino remarks, these "methodological stumbles" can yield "substantive insights."[35] They help us discover what matters most to participants and what is really at stake in any setting. Defense mechanisms, particularly when covert, are not only indicative of something else happening; they often *are* the main data points. They offer "leads" to what is especially valued, sacred, or central in a context.[36] As such, they can illuminate key field dynamics and help us see how participants make sense of their world. Like other forms of apparently odd field phenomena, covert defenses are routine products (*not* by-products) of the fields and organizations themselves.[37]

Second, there is nothing more frustrating for a field researcher than feeling enmeshed in a social web without fully understanding it. For instance, we can catch ourselves repeatedly glossing over certain aspects of our background, such as our ethnicity and nationality, to facilitate data collection, without quite grasping why we do that. Thus, being able to recognize the flavors of defense we ourselves might exhibit is key to helping us realize what we are going through, despite ourselves. It is precisely because covert defense mechanisms are collective habits so difficult to pinpoint, and so easy to mimic, that they prove hard to decipher.

We are all social beings, and most of us aim for some degree of acceptance in the communities we join or study; we are therefore quick to pick up on what makes our lives in these collectives smoother.[38] A good fieldworker strives "to get as close to a set of individuals as possible" and "to see that they are aligned against some others that are around."[39] Those others include field researchers, and we can therefore unintentionally end up defending a field *against* ourselves. By this, I mean that we can develop field-specific habits that buffer us from seeing potential patterns that we would otherwise intuit in a field.

Our learned field habits (including mimicking field participants' covert defenses) render us social, yet they can also prevent any genuine social inquiry. Taking the process of research itself as a concomitant object of inquiry in any scholarly pursuit becomes a necessity. The ethnographer Florence

Weber captures this necessity when rhetorically asking, "When you watch yourself work, do you still work the same way?" She then adds, "this kind of splitting is a necessity for ethnographers or sociologists, it's even a constitutive element of their craft."[40] We cannot omit that step of self-reflection if we want to fully grasp field dynamics.[41]

By splitting, analyzing, and categorizing experiences of resistance, I hope this book will better equip field researchers to do their work. It is important for us as fieldworkers to know about the flavors of these defenses, both to identify them in a field and to recognize them in our own behaviors. In short, a stronger fluency in these forms of defense can serve as a diagnostic tool in our scholarly explorations and a developmental strategy for ourselves.

Many examples discussed in this book come from my own field experience. Without a doubt, I found it easier to develop the cases I knew best and could contextualize, rather than relying on other sources. "Confessional tales" therefore hold an important, though not singular, place in this book.[42] Such a choice also allowed me to see better how resistance has been a persistent theme throughout my research.

It is often hard for us to provide coherence to our "puddle jumping" academic trajectories as they unfold.[43] This is even truer when conducting studies, like I do, in field settings that are often located at the margins of the mainstream and can separately be viewed by my colleagues as strange.[44] But my trajectory makes increasingly clear sense to me. Twists and turns, as well as haphazard encounters, are certainly partly responsible for what I do. Nonetheless, like for other fieldworkers, there are recurring reasons which "sustain my attention long enough to see a study through," despite "never show[ing] themselves in print."[45]

The Interloper surfaces some of the reasons or threads that have sustained, and continue to sustain, my focus. As the sociologist Brooke Harrington writes, "beneath the unique features of each researcher-participant relationship lie social psychological regularities . . . in which researchers continually explore variations on core interpersonal themes."[46] In many cases, I suspect that melting down field defenses is part of the reasons and recurring themes that infuse my assorted inquiries.

Without drawing causal inferences too directly, I speculate that growing up and identifying as gay in a mostly straight family positioned me well to have to repeatedly melt down an ever-shifting set of defenses (see coda).[47] Like the historian Allan Bérubé's constant need to "cross boundaries" as a gay youth, I too faced social barriers that I needed to push.[48] Being frequently at the margins (also as a religious minority and the child of foreign-born parents) probably provided me with a fluency at juggling defense mechanisms.[49] Thus, explaining how this grappling with field resistance is woven throughout my various pursuits helps tie them together while, importantly, shedding light on the broader significance of such resistance for other fieldworkers in their own settings.

Ultimately, the goal of this book is not to provide an exhaustive typology of field defenses, their comprehensive implications for interlopers, or what they universally mean to field participants. Instead, my goal is to draw other field researchers' attention to forms of resistance, and to do so by detailing ideal types of defenses, the unique challenges and opportunities they create for fieldworkers, as well as both what they can teach us about the fields that give rise to them and about ourselves.[50] Studying defense mechanisms aimed at preventing interlopers' access highlights not only that our research pursuits can be bumpy. It also shows that we should document, relish, and reflect (not merely complain) when stumbling over these bumps.[51] Even if they seem to sometimes stall our progress, bumps are what make us realize the relief of the terrain.

Finally, this book is not written for method fanatics or academic gatekeepers.[52] My reviewing and editorial experiences suggest that the casualties of what is sometimes labeled the "methods police" are way too costly to justify its continued existence. Of course, ensuring that studies are properly designed and conducted are preconditions of their acceptance and dissemination. Yet a study's methodological scaffolding should rarely be the sole center of a general readership's attention; the findings per se are what make studies so intriguing to most of us. In that sense, rather than a methodological blueprint for conducting proper field research, this book is meant more as a travel companion for all fieldworkers, in academia and beyond.

While I can imagine the book's main audience being aspiring and established ethnographers, organizational scholars, and sociologists, I can also see many other readers relating to its materials. Whether we study fields as part of our academic lives, immerse ourselves in them simply out of curiosity, or navigate foreign settings by necessity, we all are to some extent fieldworkers at heart. Regardless of the contexts we inhabit, most of us are curious about our environments and the societies we live in. This book is an invitation to all fieldworkers and fellow interlopers to continue finding ways to examine other people's lives and pause a bit more when presumably "failing" to succeed.

Many published field accounts just summarize in one or two sentences the resistance encountered in the field. Yet overcoming field obstacles is inherent to any field inquiry and analyzing such obstacles can deliver key lessons.[53] While some researchers acknowledge explicitly the value of these obstacles, few delve extensively into such resistance.[54] The rare researchers who do reflexively analyze such resistance along the way or retrospectively see immense benefits in the exercise.[55]

My hope is that this book will offer the impetus and framework to start analyzing field resistance as it unfolds—even before "access" materializes—as well as provide solace and companionship to all derailed, misguided, seemingly lost, and even bruised fieldworkers. Field inquiries are often more rewarding and, ultimately, worthwhile when we don't just overcome hurdles but also understand and make sense of them.

CHAPTER ONE

Obstructing Access

FINALLY, I HAD SECURED an invite: I would be able to attend the meeting of clinical anatomists in New York State charged with collecting whole-body donations for their medical schools. Or so I thought. Having been invited to attend by several people, I showed up the day of the event feeling very upbeat, because this was the main arena for them to collectively discuss the challenges they faced in securing cadavers—a topic I had, by then, been studying for several years. Midway through the meeting, however, a member successfully put forth a motion that prevented me from attending all subsequent meetings.

Rarely had I been caught so off guard in my research in the field! I remember looking at the other attendees, almost in shock that this member would publicly attempt such a bold move. The room grew quiet for a few seconds before the vote was cast, and, in that moment, I still felt hopeful. But by a show of hands, a majority of attendees voted in favor of the proposal (probably out of loyalty to this influential member). An even longer, even more awkward silence ensued: my memory of the rest of the meeting is a bit elusive.

The way in which the obstruction occurred was particularly stinging. The person who wanted me out of the room asked me—in a hyperbolic tone, and in front of his attentive peers—whether I intended to study him. Coming from an anatomist used to dissect cadavers, I found the question rather ironic. Did he himself not study *others* constantly, not to mention dead ones, in his anatomy classes? My study felt rather unobtrusive compared to his daily practice. Regardless, the question was not rhetorical, and my explanations failed to convince. I was branded persona non grata at the committee: never to return to its regular gatherings.[1]

This would be the first and only meeting of the New York group of clinical anatomists that I attended. I was not escorted out that day, but it felt like it. Returning to my field notes from that meeting, I can see how sparse they were and how hard it was for me to focus on my task after this blow. It only took a quick vote for me to no longer be able to access that key locus of the field's activity. The door had literally shut.

But what I was only beginning to learn is that such an obstacle offers its own crucial insights for researchers. In fact—as I was to discover—there was a precedent for these anatomists to keep me out, and perhaps even a good one, in their eyes. Over the past decades, these anatomists had faced what they perceived as increased "competition" from new entrants seeking to secure cadavers for a broad range of uses. While the total number of donations remained steady, the demand for cadavers and body parts was rapidly growing. During that time, opportunities to cut moral corners to get as many bodies as possible flourished—for instance, by securing a donation from a next of kin rather than the deceased prior to death. What resists in a field is often real. Only by repeatedly pushing at the defense, however, can one chip away at it—and start to see what it might reveal.

It would take me some time to realize that preventing outsiders from gaining physical access to their whole-body programs was a common strategy for clinical anatomists in academically housed programs to maintain the purity of their work.[2] The key way in which they envisioned their professional mandate entailed always keeping the perimeter of operations impermeable. They did their utmost to keep people from "trespassing" on their geography—whether that geography boiled down to their offices (generally in basements), their hospitals, the wider cities and state in which they collected donations, or their New York State meeting. What I had imagined as a simple request (i.e., the idea of observing a meeting) likely triggered a reaction that proved telling in many ways.[3] The collective obstruction they exhibited echoed an actual or imagined fear of intrusions that structured their interactions, norms, and habits in more ways than I ever imagined.

I probably should have known better, since my first encounter with such obstruction from clinical anatomists took place in Las Vegas a few years earlier. Like in the case of the New York meeting, a few anatomists I had grown close to invited me to join them for the event. By that point, it had been more than a year since I had started my study of the US commerce in human cadavers, and I was gradually learning about its intricacies.[4] In particular, several highly publicized cases of donations gone wrong had sent waves throughout the profession and triggered internal discussions on its code of conduct.

Their annual conference was set in Las Vegas and seemed to be the place these discussions converged. From my evening flight's window, the Las Vegas strip looked magical and promising. When I saw the strip for the first time as my plane landed, the city seemed—to me—full of hope. Clinical anatomists from all over the United States were converging for their annual meeting, and I could not dream of a better occasion to gain access to the nearly one hundred academic whole-body donation programs represented there.

Also arriving in town for the conference were my two "favorite" anatomists, Jessica and Brad: favorite, in part, because they generously and invariably answered my emails as well as fielded my questions on the technicalities of their line of work. Jessica was arriving from the West Coast, Brad from the East. "It will be a great party," Jessica had promised. "Imagine piña coladas all night long around a pool! You shouldn't miss it," Brad insisted. Both were also looking forward to finally meeting me face-to-face. How could I say no?

But it wasn't the idea of a cocktail party near a pool that excited me most about Las Vegas, nor what made the visit seem so promising. With hundreds of people gathering for the American Association of Clinical Anatomists annual meeting, the crowd would be a magnet for my ongoing inquiry into their evolving profession—or at least, I thought so. Most of the US whole-body donation program representatives attend and even have their own reserved slot in the program, one elusively titled "Anatomical Services business meeting." All the big names in the field of body donation would be present at the session. And, best of all, the meeting's organizer had kindly allocated me five minutes to explain the research I was doing and how attendees might help.

To make life easier for all those involved at the Anatomical Services business meeting, I brought printouts that summarized my study, as well as a minisurvey (a few short questions) printed on small forms: i.e., a study recruitment flyer. These minisurveys would allow those in attendance wishing to help to fill in their names and drop the form in a box while exiting the meeting. Like any good social scientist, I had pretested the form on some insiders; I was confident it would yield enough answers to instigate follow-ups with those who agreed to talk, and for me to learn more about their programs. In the days before the meeting, I could already imagine an endless number of doors opening.

Surprisingly, the party was as memorable as Jessica and Brad had promised. They took turns guiding me through the crowd as drinks flowed. The flickering of the lights off the pool water, the palm trees, and the DJ all made for a fantastic evening. Brad seemed to know everybody—from Seattle to Florida, ranging from young to old anatomists—and he was eager to draw me into his informal banter. Similarly, Jessica had a constant stream of anatomists come salute her. She seemed respected by many attendees and easily approachable. Topics of conversations ranged from kids and vacations to more business-like matters. *Had Jessica heard about this donation case run amuck in a program in New Jersey? What were Brad's thoughts on this new body preservation method? Had they figured-out a way to better track body parts?* I relished in these stories.

Several people I met that evening told me they would be at the business meeting the next day and would love to talk again. They seemed engaged and offered to open the doors of their program. After perhaps one drink too many, I decided to call it a night and head to bed. "What a great way to start this conference and learn so much about donations in just one spot," I recall thinking. Las Vegas was truly living up to its promise.

The next day, more than a hundred people sat in the Grand Ballroom I of the Green Valley Ranch Resort and Spa. The meeting was large and already included some of the people who would later vote me out in New York. Like any typical academic meeting I had attended, noise and even laughter filled the room, and everyone seemed eager to catch up before getting started. Many of the people I had met at the party were in the room. They greeted me warmly. I could spot Jessica near the front rows chatting with colleagues. Back a few rows, Brad was surrounding by a coterie of aficionados. The midafternoon meeting was one of the last that day. The transition to the less formal program had not yet begun, but an evident giddiness in the room suggested that attendees were already thinking about the social events (and parties) soon to come.

I was feeling good about my upcoming presentation and had even remembered to bring a small box to collect my forms. I simply needed to explain my research design, distribute my forms, and have those interested in me learning more about their anatomical donation programs write their name, location, and email or phone contact, so I could follow up. My request seemed minimal: I was interested in talking to them to learn more about the hopes and challenges they saw in their work—a first step towards a more in-depth examination of their practices. My favorite anatomists smiled as I gave my short talk. I could see my flyers blanketing the room, and I sent a few more down to some spots which had been missed, to ensure full coverage on ending my pitch. Other speakers then came to the stand and updated the crowd on other topics related to anatomical donations. Within less than an hour, the organizer thanked everyone for coming, closed the session, and reminded participants to drop the flyers I had distributed in the box near the ballroom exit.

As I stood guard near my box, the large crowd trickled out. A few people I had met at the party walked right past the box, despite having assured me the evening before that they were game to chat and even perhaps allow me to visit their programs. One even came up to me to congratulate me, but when asked whether he might entertain my request for more information, he told me he would think about it. A sense of gloom suddenly grew. Did I come to Las Vegas for nothing? The noise started to abate and the few remaining attendees left the room. The ballroom was now empty except for the organizers. Members of the resort's cleaning crew dashed in to prepare for the next day's session. My box was empty!

Out of more than a hundred attendees, not one had filled out my flyer. Of course, I could try to convince myself that some had kept it and would reach out later, since it included my contact information. However, many flyers littered the now empty chairs. Indeed, I watched the cleaners now tossing them away. I recall angrily trashing the small box I had painstakingly constructed. Had the shiny Las Vegas lights deceived me?

After the ballroom debacle, I passed the palm trees and pool again on my way to my room to recuperate from the disappointment. Like returning from an expedition without a prize, I could not help but see my entire time spent in Las Vegas as a failure. Any memories of the party were now tainted. The feeling of having a door slammed in my face was particularly painful. What had I done wrong? Why did these anatomists block my inquiry despite seeming so welcoming up-front?

The closing doors, setting up of roadblocks, and prevention of trespassing did not only concern me. Those behaviors were also aimed at safeguarding the sanctity of whole-body donation programs from *other* intruders, primarily those they called "body-brokers." Both Brad and Jessica had used that term, but I had not yet fully realized the existential threat it conveyed.

In the moment, obstructed access might seem like a major annoyance for fieldworkers. It nonetheless teaches us a lot about the challenges faced by the clinical anatomists charged with collecting whole-body donations for their medical schools. Obstructions, like other forms of field defense, can suggest a paranoia of intrusion that is more indicative of the dynamics in a field than the intruder per se. I wish I had known at that time not to take the door-slamming personally.

Unfortunately, I blamed myself and squandered that initial opportunity to make sense of this field's dynamics. It would take another act of defense (i.e., being voted out of the New York meeting) to better understand what such obstructions revealed about the world of whole-body donations.

For decades, the work of clinical anatomists had been evolving. And it was this context that, in part, set the stage for why clinical anatomists were so adamant to obstruct access. The obstruction, then, was an access all of its own. Obstructing proved a window into, rather than a barrier to, their world.

Both medical education and scientific research require human cadavers. These traditionally have been procured by "whole-body donation programs," which often operate in conjunction with established institutions like medical schools. But, starting in the 1980s, the staff of US whole-body donation programs noticed something new: independent ventures— with reassuring names like Science Care and the LifeLegacy Foundation—also started to secure specimens, and offered them to medical schools willing to pay for their services.[5]

Taking advantage of an opportunity created by the legislation governing the procurement and use of cadavers, such new ventures began competing alongside more established, academically housed programs for donations. While academic programs acquired and used cadavers locally, independent ventures tended to acquire and send cadavers nationally. The ventures actively recruited donors in states with high concentrations of retirees, like Arizona and Florida, and then sent their specimens across the country. By the early 2000s, these large ventures became dominant actors in the trade of human cadavers. Before, medical schools had always struggled to find an adequate supply of cadavers to train their future physicians and other health professionals.[6] But now, thanks to these new national ventures, such schools could finally access a new and plentiful source of specimens.

Yet a consortium of medical schools in New York State made sure no cadavers from these independent ventures entered the state. Despite legislation allowing for the movement of cadavers across state lines, archival data on cadaver acquisition in New York (soon after these ventures grew in size) shows that in-state programs essentially obstructed almost every ventures' activity in the state. For example, of the cadavers secured in 2007 by all users located in New York State, only thirty-one (1.8 percent) came from outside the state.[7] And these few out-of-state cadavers came from another academically housed program in New Jersey, not from independent ventures. Thus, despite the broad availability of specimens from ventures nationwide, almost all the cadavers acquired by New York State medical schools that year (and in subsequent ones) were procured locally.

A New York State association, which brought together most large in-state medical schools' anatomists, orchestrated this obstruction, just as that same association would one day vote me out of their meeting. This association defended itself against the rise of independent ventures by preventing them from entering medical schools' perimeter of activity. Because association members feared that market dynamics would taint the commerce in cadavers, they selectively offered each other specimens (by trading cadavers in the state) to discourage members from going on the open (out-of-state) "market." These exchanges were complicated to set up and perform, but they ultimately prevented ventures from getting a foothold in New York State.

By de facto obstructing access, the association not only limited these ventures' activities. They also hoped, more broadly, to thwart the commercialization of the US trade in

cadavers. Indeed, the key issue for which the medical association's anatomists were fighting was the moralization of trade
in bodily goods. Through its actions, the association was therefore taking a moral stand. Might this stand, I would later
speculate, be worth them preventing me from observing
their discussions?

Interlopers in the Trade of Human Cadavers

I was blissfully unaware of clinical anatomists' raging moral
battles when I became intrigued by whole body donations. Initially, my interest was piqued by the hushed tone used by a
friend completing a pathology residency to describe a space
near his office being used to house cadavers. But, after Las
Vegas, I undertook a closer examination of the evolving profession of clinical anatomy. Soon, the obstruction I had faced
forced me into a greater understanding, and I learned that the
growth in the trade of cadavers (in the mid-2000s) helped
explain why the New York State association of medical schools
was vehemently opposed to seeing independent ventures operate alongside their members.

As early as the eighteenth and nineteenth centuries, cadaver
procurement in the United States operated mostly "outside of
the legal process or in the shadows of law" and was commonly
referred to as "body-snatching."[8] Shady connections and informal networks were the backbone of these activities. Medical
training required cadavers, yet no legal framework existed to
ensure their procurement. And so medical schools, in most
cases, outsourced the dirty work to external parties who were
assumed to be held to "lower" moral standards than their
patrons. Those actually responsible for procuring corpses
often resorted to disinterring cadavers or paying others to do
so.[9] But eventually, legislative action to regulate the cadaver

trade provided those involved with a new legal basis for their pursuit.

Starting in 1968, the Uniform Anatomical Gift Act (UAGA), gradually adopted by every US state, formed a legal framework for such trades.[10] The act specified, for instance, how to obtain a donor's consent and respect the decedents' wishes. A 1987 revision of the Uniform Anatomical Gift Act, also enacted by most US states, made it a felony to "knowingly, for valuable consideration, purchase or sell a [body] part for transplantation or therapy, if removal of the part is intended to occur after the death of the decedent." The revision excluded, however, "the reasonable payment for the removal, processing, disposal, preservation, quality control, storage, transportation, or implantation of a part" by specimen users.[11] This 1987 provision (or what some might label as a loophole) enabled independent ventures to exist, since it enshrined a new business model: allowing them to legally charge for their services.

In parallel, the demand for cadavers was now constantly on the rise. While medical schools have always been the main users of specimens, the growth of related medical fields and continuing medical education suddenly added to the demand. Besides physicians, individuals training in reconstructive dentistry and osteopathic medicine also needed jaws and joints to hone their skills. Moreover, large manufacturers of medical devices were increasingly offering new products, and these needed to be tested in their development stages with cadavers or body parts. These manufacturers also encouraged professionals to come and learn the intricacies of their new devices (in their deployment stages) in high-end facilities, again using cadavers or body parts.[12]

These combined developments explain why, by the early 2000s, more than a dozen independent ventures—both for- and nonprofit organizations, yet neither affiliated with any research or higher education institution—emerged to cater to these demands. Las Vegas, then, was not only a location for clinical anatomists' annual meeting. It was also, for instance, a hub for physicians to learn new stem-implant techniques, using torsos procured by ventures, and to practice manipulating other medical devices necessitating alternate body parts.

Gradually, the scale of independent ventures' operations made them key players in the field of body donations. And this, in turn, prompted an existential fear among clinical anatomists working in medical schools. The anatomists worried that these new players would taint the field—the acquiring and trade of human cadavers—with commerce. But they also feared that the new ventures would capture a large slice of a limited overall supply of donations.

By the mid-2000s, in fact, the two largest US independent ventures were already each securing several thousand donations per year. Meanwhile, at best, the most successful academically housed programs were securing each year only several hundred. And these changes were occurring in a total supply of whole-body donations estimated in 2006 at approximately twenty thousand per year in the United States.[13]

So, the high numbers of donations reported by ventures made many anatomists uneasy. The uneven scale of operations between academic programs and ventures—namely, local versus national—only added to anatomists' fears.[14] Many clinical anatomists were afraid that their ability to continue securing enough donations for their students might be in jeopardy. The large ventures' meteoric rise was the "elephant" in the Las Vegas ballroom the elephant I had bumped into with my earnest efforts to get the anatomists to tell me more about their (threatened) work.[15]

Medical Schools' Obstruction

Faced with this perceived existential threat, medical schools throughout the United States tried to take action, but the New York State schools were probably the best organized. They did not overtly forbid these ventures access to their territory (since they could not legally do so). Instead, they ensured that their members would not need to interact with ventures, de facto obstructing ventures from operating in the state.

Nine medical schools that had historically supplied their academic peers with specimens became the promoters of this defense strategy. All nine schools were part of the Anatomical Committee of the Associated Medical Schools of New York (AMSNY). AMSNY was a consortium of public and private medical schools, and its anatomical committee (with eighteen schools represented) aimed to improve whole-body donation practices. Both Brad and Jessica, not located in New York State, knew about these efforts and on several occasions spoke very highly of this committee—the exact committee that voted me out.

Since its inception, the committee had hosted a yearly coordination meeting to discuss cadaver supply-and-demand challenges. It also encouraged schools with excess donations (e.g., SUNY Upstate Medical Center) to transfer some specimens to those lacking sufficient donations (e.g., Mount Sinai School of Medicine). While the committee always encouraged transfers among its members, it started also asking members to voluntarily report any cadaver transfers. Rapidly, the committee informally agreed upon an annual transfer scheme to ensure that all in-state medical schools (even those not represented in the committee) would be able to secure donations in-state. Thanks to this coordination, the University of Rochester, for example, knew exactly how many and to what schools to transfer its excess specimens. These schools no longer needed to reach out to independent ventures like Science Care or the LifeLegacy Foundation.

Thus, my empty survey box in Las Vegas proved to be, in some ways, a canary in the mine. Besides indicating a baseline resistance to being studied by outsiders, it also likely offered an early signal of participants' deepest fears of physical incursions into their world and of the typical way they handled such threats: i.e., by blocking access. It foreshadowed the well-designed choreography of obstruction that the committee could seamlessly reproduce year after year. It also illuminated some of the key moral battles raging in the field around proper ways to secure and use donations.

This is why it is important to pay attention to patterns of resistance that interlopers—like me—can trigger. Such patterns, if properly noted, may reveal the intricate meanings that participants project into such defenses. Obstructing my access was fully normalized in this setting. Here, clinical anatomists viewed obstructing as a moral crusade against independent ventures. These meanings are precisely what field researchers aim to uncover.

Obstructing is perhaps the most noticeable and powerful resistance mechanism a field can exhibit in light of an interloper's access attempt. Obstructing creates a solid wall against most intrusions and leaves those trying to enter with little to work with. Depending on the setting, the precise flavor of the obstruction will vary, but ultimately the result is the same. When prevented from accessing a field, the potential interloper can only back off, at least temporarily, and ponder a next move.

My emotional reaction to the empty survey box in Las Vegas crystallized this feeling of powerlessness. Yet it also fueled my desire to find an unguarded door. Obstructed interlopers retreat momentarily, in the hope of a future success. The sense of failure can prove crushing *and* energizing, since the emotional rollercoaster is often worthwhile. Field obstruction generally goes beyond blocking entry to ethnographers like me. Obstruction captures a field's core tension, one that can shift widely.[16] How field participants react to interlopers—those attempting to probe into their inner workings—provides early warnings of what to expect when delving deeper into an inquiry.

Let me share two similarly telling yet otherwise different examples of field obstruction and the contrasted underlying meanings they might reveal. Both are set in apparently related settings (a crime lab and a medical examiner's office), and in both cases the researchers faced obstructions. Yet each flavor of obstruction points to a very different field dynamic that cannot be predicted by merely cataloguing the symptomatic form of defense.

Upon first trying to conduct an ethnography of crime labs, the ethnographer Beth Bechky met with different lab directors. All expressed interest in her project. Yet all ultimately declined to participate, "either because their [overseeing] agency head said no, or they were unwilling to ask."[17] One director added that he was not sure who the new police chief would be and that he could not take the risk of making such a request on Bechky's behalf. Such a perceived impossibility to help because of others' imagined preferences, however, augured one of Bechky's study's key findings: namely, that crime lab scientists viewed themselves as members of an occupation "captive" to the criminal justice world or constantly "responding to law enforcement expectations and requests."[18] Thus, the way scientists justified up-front their obstruction to the researcher made clear that such captivity was top of their mind. In deferring to law enforcement—and, more

specifically, judges, prosecutors, lawyers, and police officers—
when vetting interlopers, these scientists were openly sharing
what most structured their days: namely, this constant antici-
pation of potential oversight on their work.

Similarly, when trying to access medical examiners' offices,
the sociologist Stefan Timmermans also recalls that the first
examiner he contacted proved obstructive. But the examiner
asked him two questions as well before deciding to block
access: how many people worked above and below him? Once
this examiner understood that Timmermans was literally
alone (without a real "boss" or any direct reports), he dismissed his request: he understood, it seemed, that the political
liability of his refusal was low. (In the examiner's view, the
refusal impacted few others, so the social fallout to saying no
would be easily contained.) As Timmermans recounts, "this
encounter taught me a hard lesson about the contested nature
of investigating suspicious deaths."[19] The flavor of this obstruction was indicative of medical examiners' extreme attentive-
ness to the *political* costs of their decisions, whether allowing
an interloper to enter a field or listing a cause of death on a
certificate. Timmermans' study then goes on to document the
contested ways of classifying causes of death, and how examiners weigh the political costs of doing so.

The crystallizing power of these flavors of obstruction
points to powerful and distinctive (future) insights revealed by
each study. Obstructing is not always indicative of the same
kind of tension within a field. Instead, forms of resistance
(such as obstructing) are symptomatic and indicative of a tension that often still requires more probing to be fully revealed.
Beyond the forms of resistance per se that we encounter, their
unique flavors are what make them so telling. The more attentive we are to these resistance patterns, the faster we learn
what's truly at stake in our fields.

Obstructing's Implications for Interlopers

When hitting a wall of obstruction, tenacity is needed to break through. We constantly need to imagine our next steps in order to attempt to reenter through another door. The temptation is to give up. Yet, at the same time, we can often sense that something more is at stake, since we view the obstruction as a growing sign of the inquiry's necessity. And the feeling of being on the "right path," even if others might see it as wrong, fuels this persistence.

At the time of my study, the New York State committee dealing with whole-body donations had many members I had individually spoken to or met once the study finally got rolling. Through word of mouth and private introduction, I had managed by then to snowball from my Baltimore contact to interview a fair number of clinical anatomists across the country, including in New York State.[20] Some level of obstruction, then, I had overcome in the years since Las Vegas. And yet, as noted earlier, when I was brought into the room of the New York committee, the members looked me over and voted me out. Tenacity seemed the only way forward. I suspect that many other "obstructed" researchers develop a similarly thick skin in response to field defenses and must reboot their inquiries multiple times.

Another implication for interlopers faced with obstruction is that they often do not fully know what is behind the wall. They feel something is peculiar, but what triggers the defense can sometimes be beyond their current imagination and reach, given that it is off-limits. In the case of this committee's behavior, I only learned much later about the many layers behind the obstruction attempt. As I gathered more interviews, field notes, and archives, it gradually became obvious that the New York anatomists were protecting themselves against the independent ventures' entry into the state. Yet the fervor with which they barred me—a lone researcher, unaffiliated with any venture— from entering the field was more puzzling.

One of the main new opportunities for interlopers faced with contemporary fields trying to obstruct their access is that many activities are increasingly digital and spread out geographically. They occur not only in one given physical place but also through a treasure trove of online and electronic interactions.[21] Solidly walling off a crime lab or a medical examiner's office is probably easier than trying to do so with a disseminated space generating rich digital traces within and between locations.

For example, while I was kicked out of the New York State anatomists' meetings, I slipped back into the field through a crack: locating a scanned record of all their cadaver "trades" held at the New York State Department of Health. (The department required programs to report the number of specimens they secured, the origins of these specimens, and the number of specimens used.) The level of specificity found in these records blew me away. Some medical schools were not only reporting the number of cadavers sent or acquired but also breaking down their "inventory" into subcategories (such as torso, knees, legs, and feet) in what seemed like an overzealous attempt to comply with state-level regulations. The digital archive was, in some ways, even more informative than the regular meetings, and obstructing my access to it proved more difficult.

I secured these rich data on procurement and use of cadavers in New York State via a Freedom of Information Act (FOIA) request. And, consequently, I did discover an anomaly. The numbers reported by the medical school employing the person who had organized my expulsion at the meeting did not match up. In short, the number of reported cadavers used at the school did not equal the reported number of those received that given year—leaving open the possibility that they had "supplemented" their local (in-state) allocation by other means or that their accounting was slightly off.

I never fully got to the bottom of this mismatch. But it's worth noting that the most energetic obstructers are likely those who have the most to lose with a disruption to the status-quo.[22] Obstruction is probably their second-best option; that is, when they cannot fully hide their activities—another defense mechanism detailed in the next chapter.

Even after publishing the main results of my study on the commerce of human cadavers, I continued for close to a decade to make annual FOIA requests to monitor the procurement and use of cadavers in New York State. I may not have known what I was looking for, but I had learned how to melt the defense of a field that had stubbornly resisted me. Each new wave of released data felt like a small victory. Every year, I awaited the new data, in order to comb the records for oddities, particularly for anomalies in the anatomist's home institution reporting. I never again noticed anything strange, and the initial blip that caught my eye might have simply been a reporting error.

Nonetheless, I felt an obligation to monitor these ongoing trades in cadavers. I had perhaps internalized the moral crusade that many clinical anatomists had described in my interviews with them. The combination of distance and involvement is always a tricky balance in field research.[23] My social proximity to clinical anatomists (most of them employed, like me, by a university) had probably made me more attentive to their fears; this proximity made me wary of independent ventures' unchecked expansion.

In an uncanny way, then, the former interloper was now the one monitoring intrusions. The person previously snooping around in search of access gradually morphed into a protector of the field's central cultural norms and beliefs. This transformation is a testimony to the power of fields to enroll strangers, even unconsciously, into their most sacred pursuits.

CHAPTER TWO

Hiding from View

THE DAY METROPOLITAN AIRPORT'S State Police briefly detained one of the graduate students enrolled in my doctoral seminar was not my proudest moment as an educator. The email informing me of the unfolding of events arrived in the early hours of a Saturday morning. As part of a class assignment in this seminar on field research methodologies, I had asked students to conduct one prearranged interview with a Transportation Security Administration (TSA) screening officer and to observe screening activities from the large airport halls (prior to passing security checks). Through these exercises, as well as writing memos and field notes to later share with the class, students would hopefully learn how to overcome the numerous pitfalls of conducting field research. Being detained was not a pitfall I had in mind.

My ongoing relation with TSA officials, particularly a person I will call Jack, led me to believe that the observations would be a no-brainer since the agency was helping us secure the interviews.[1] Jack had been my dream field contact. He was several decades older than I was and offered the kind of nurturing support that an ideal father figure can provide. I often marveled at how attentively he listened during our exchanges before offering ways to help. In addition, his pressed suit and shirt, brightened by an official TSA pin, impressed me. In short, Jack's presence suggested that all would go for the best.

That Saturday morning, however, this student, Hannah, rapidly warned the entire class and me that the TSA assignment was riskier than expected. I was perhaps a bit too taken by Jack's welcome and wrongly assumed that airport halls were semipublic spaces. I should have, of course, given advance notice to Jack about the observational component of the exercise.

My misstep was unforgiveable. But the detaining of this student underlined that hiding from public view—that is, hiding from an outside observer—called for constant craft and efforts. Crucially, this episode also highlighted TSA's familiarity with such hiding dynamics and its unease with being seen, and, more broadly, it showed how hiding can be deployed as a field defense mechanism.

Unbeknown to her at the time, Hannah had stepped into what would later emerge to be a key topic of concern to TSA members. I uncovered this in a study that I co-led shortly after at the agency: the tension revolved around the visibility/invisibility of TSA staff to the outside world and to higher-ups.[2] In a context of potential security threats and intense public scrutiny of its operations, TSA employees were more likely to hide than to disclose what they were doing. Through her inquisitive behavior, Hannah had brushed up against a core threat for the agency's members, that of being seen, and had activated a hiding defense, which this chapter will analyze.

Because the shape of a field's core threat differs drastically from one field to another, the nature of the field's reaction also varies widely. While fears of intrusion generated obstruction from clinical anatomists, fear of being seen elicited hiding behaviors on the part of TSA employees. Participants' unique responses to an interloper's attempt to "access" both fields yield sharply contrasted yet very informative data on how field participants think.

Hannah was generally one of the first students to turn in assignments. Not surprisingly, she headed to Metropolitan airport almost immediately after reading my instructions to interview officers and observe the checkpoints.[3] She then explained what happened: "I went to Terminal B . . . where I found that the screening points at each end were significantly more visible [than in Terminal C] from nearby public benches." She went on to specify, "I observed for over an hour at the busy U.S. Airways end. At that point, however, desiring to be a 'good social scientist,' I thought I'd spend another half-hour at the opposite end—an Air Canada screening point that I had observed was much less busy (comparative study and all that, of course!). This was a tactical error."

The second vantage point proved much more exposed for her. Hannah continued, "Although I had spent more than an hour and escaped notice at the other checkpoint, I was spotted and considered suspicious within about 20 minutes by the Air Canada screeners who alas, as noted, had little else to do, given a much lighter passenger load. Lesson #1: Pick a busy checkpoint. Lesson #2: If you think you have been 'noticed,' you have." She went on to spell out her fear and the worst-case scenario, "I don't think it would have been wise of me to leave at that point, as a sketch of me might have wound up in State Police offices somewhere or on a terrorist watch website."

Her closing words to the class were far wiser than my instructions. She politely wrote, "I expect everyone else will be cleverer than I was about avoiding detection."

A state police officer first confronted Hannah, sternly, when he noticed her lingering near the security checkpoints in the hall and asked what she was doing. His abrupt appearance did not bode well. She told him she had come to the airport to interview a TSA officer and to conduct observations. Luckily, she was able to produce a form on university letterhead that she had printed for the interview. (Equipping students with this letter was my only redeeming act in this minifiasco.) After the officer and four TSA employees encircled her and examined her driver's license, they started inquiring with their higher-ups about what to do next. During that time, Hannah waited cautiously for an outcome.

The small group "deliberated her fate," as Hannah put it in her message to us, for about fifteen minutes. Finally, they gave her a green light to proceed. Still, despite being authorized to continue, she left at once. I have often wondered how long the deliberations might have taken had she not been a fair-skinned woman.

Upon receiving her email, I immediately wrote to Jack to inform him of what had happened and apologized for not having looped him in. His good-humored reply underscored that he had seen much worse events in his long career, which had started in the Coast Guard. This episode barely registered as an annoyance on his radar. He thanked me for informing him and threw in a few typical words of encouragement. No other student was detained.

Nonetheless, for the TSA personnel caught off guard, "being seen" proved disturbing. This agency under the aegis of the Department of Homeland Security was highly uncomfortable with being observed. It was not the first time that its staff members dealt with such surveillance. Again, that unease was built on and revealed solid foundations.

Fields trying to hide their inner workings from outsiders are nothing new. Many organizations, for instance, try to hide their proprietary knowledge or other "trade" secrets to ensure that they maintain their competitive positions in markets. Yet because we never know what remains hidden, the extent to which hiding occurs across fields proves difficult to assess.

That said, one would expect those dealing with security issues (like TSA staff) to be more likely than others to hide their activities. There are at least two reasons for that. First, security threats tend to be diffuse and often call for extra caution on the part of insiders. (There is always a temptation to believe that the less outsiders know, the safer life will be for insiders.) Second, even if outsiders are well intentioned, they might inadvertently reveal an idiosyncrasy that could create a vulnerability. This risk exists because outsiders are not aware of what needs to remain hidden. Identifying and assessing a level of threat requires an expertise that they often lack; this is why police officers tend to trust only their own when conducting their work.[4] Under such circumstances, organizations dealing with security issues are likely to prefer to hide most of what they do, until cornered into a disclosure.

The extent to which security organizations try to hide their activities is well illustrated by how the British Ministry of Defense reacted to an ethnographer's presence. When Mark de Rond engaged in a study of British military doctors in Afghanistan, he did so after having been courted for years by a high-ranking medical officer, who was intrigued by the idea of shedding a brighter light on how doctors operate in war zones. At the study's completion, this same officer asked to read a draft of the resulting book manuscript and then suddenly "expressed concern," even to the point of escalating the issue to his superior.[5] Now, the Ministry wanted the book's contents hidden. It opposed its publication because it "worried that the book might damage the interests of the United Kingdom internationally, seriously obstruct the promotion or protection by the United Kingdom of those interests, or endanger the safety of British citizens abroad."[6] The worries centered on the study's open description of civilian casualties.[7] Ultimately, the book went to press. But had the Ministry been more forceful or the author more vulnerable (e.g., an untenured faculty member), the attempts to hide discussions of civilian casualties might have succeeded.

In other instances, just what is being hidden can seem less clear. While the act of pulling the curtain is often easy to pinpoint, the contents behind the curtain usually remain fuzzier. In the TSA's case, what the agency was trying to hide from Hannah proved much more layered and complex than the disclosure of a single potentially damaging piece of information (like the extent of civilian casualties for the British military). Indeed, the TSA's fears went beyond the typical ones found in security organizations. They ranged from management's fear of employee theft of travelers' belongings to employees' fear of management sanctions for not following regulations.

All these elements, detailed next, coalesced, and help explain the TSA's genuine anxiety around being seen. In retrospect, these unique field dynamics justified the quick action of the state police and TSA members upon discovering Hannah in the airport hall. They also underline my initial cluelessness in sending students to observe TSA officers at checkpoints. Like foot soldiers sent to test enemy defense lines, seminar participants were headed into an unknown minefield; (minor) casualties would help us collectively decipher the terrain.

The Fear of Being Seen at TSA

The field landscape we encountered at TSA in the early 2010s was indeed unusual. Almost a decade after its inception in 2001, one of the most critical and unexpected workforce issues that

TSA faced was the recurring accusations of employee theft. Every year, travelers made a substantial number of claims that officers had stolen from their belongings. As an illustration, out of more than twelve thousand passenger claims reported nationwide to TSA in 2009, almost 60 percent concerned "passengers' property loss from checked-in baggage and at checkpoint[s]."[8]

To identify the potential culprits and protect other employees from unjust accusations, TSA managers gradually introduced heightened surveillance measures at checkpoints, installing closed-circuit television cameras. This move was part of a multimillion-dollar effort to use surveillance cameras to counter the public's perception of employee theft. As the Government Accountability Office noted, "TSA officials at airports often have to rely upon video footage to substantiate whether misconduct has occurred, such as alleged theft of a passenger's property."[9] Moreover, another government report explained that the footage could be used to review travelers' complaints and "help identify additional details of the incident, such as the identity of the screener(s) who may have been involved in the incident."[10] Consequently, installing cameras at all security checkpoints rapidly became the "best practice" advocated by TSA management across all US airports.[11]

Within years of that decision, the rise in surveillance became ubiquitous, at least, to any TSA employee who had been at the agency while the decision was being implemented. In fact, that's one of the only things screening officers wanted to talk to us about when we interviewed them.[12] The cameras above every workspace, and their utilization of different angles to observe activities, put TSA screeners' daily work under a constant managerial gaze. Aside from restrooms, few airport spaces remained out of view.

While this overexposure made screeners highly visible to their managers, it also paradoxically encouraged screeners to develop a wide range of informal invisibility practices to remain hidden from managerial view. The first time I went for a meeting with TSA representatives in their local office about conducting a study there, the secretary who communicated the location to me joked that the office was somewhat hidden. "Go past the central parking, follow the signs for the administrative building, go down a corridor, press the button near the elevator, wait, and someone will see you and come down," she explained. At that time, I hardly picked up on her use of the word hidden, but over the course of our study, we repeatedly discovered that she was not the only one "hiding" at TSA.[13]

With the growth of surveillance, the most salient perceived outcome for TSA employees was the possibility for management to notice them when they were not following standard procedure and consequently for them to undergo disciplinary action.[14] Screeners shared among themselves stories of employees caught on camera, perhaps for simply reading a newspaper when no travelers were at the checkpoints or for wearing their badge improperly (e.g., partly covered or upside down). A feeling of "Big Brother" constantly watching them soon tainted their behaviors and their relation to their employer.

By association and after several interviews that I conducted (a few years after Hannah had done hers), I also learned to be on my "best behavior" when roaming the airport grounds. In fact, I would often make mental notes of the various cameras I could spot when walking from my parking spot to my meeting points. Moreover, I made sure not to arrive too early for a meeting, since that would mean lingering perhaps a bit too long in a space that might be monitored.

In this context, screeners—and I—quickly learned to hide from cameras. The preferred, but also most difficult, way to do so was to go physically "off-camera." This could be achieved by extending scheduled breaks in less monitored areas (such as travelers' food courts) or by taking longer than needed to reach new destinations when changing checkpoints. In a telling episode, a screener who was asked to work at another checkpoint recalled "just wandering the airport" a bit and being able to "go hide someplace" before reporting to duty. The screeners relished these unmonitored moments, since they allowed them to attain a form of temporary invisibility.

I also learned firsthand, when in the field, about these attempts to go off-camera. The coffee shop that I had picked in one of the terminals to schedule my interviews always seemed deserted and its tables far apart; this, I assumed, meant we would not be bothered. Yet my initial interviewees, though they did speak openly, also seemed a bit on their guard. I attributed their attitude to my novelty in the field. With the fourth interviewee, though, we immediately hit it off. After more than an hour talking, she was the one who pointed to the cameras not too far from the coffee shop I had selected. "We are constantly observed here, it's not great," she told me. "You might want to pick another place the next time," she said with a smile. When I pressed her for suggestions, she spontaneously went down a list of several other possibilities, as though she had a clear map of where you were less seen at the airport. Based on her advice, I moved all my interviews to a location she suggested. Each time I reached that new destination, the large and lush potted plants that populate it conveyed a much more protective feeling than they ever had before.

A second and less obvious way to hide was for screeners to refrain from "sticking out," even in plain sight of cameras. The strategy entailed for them to "lie low" or "float under the radar," so managers could not fully notice and remember them. Because of a constant rotation of screeners at gates (i.e., teams were regularly recomposed), such lying low proved remarkably effective. A screener detailed how her typical day involved "not putting [herself] out there," so her boss would not recall her; instead, she pretended not to pay attention to overheard conversations among her supervisors in order "to be left alone" and remain "not known." An episode when a supervisor needed to peer at long-time employees' name-badges before greeting them hinted at the success of these invisibility strategies.

Thus, hiding became the default course of informal action for many TSA employees. And this hiding might help explain, in retrospect, why some initial interview transcripts seemed so bland. While conducting her early observations, Hannah had walked into a workplace where employees were informally obsessed with trying to hide. But, as we will see, such obsession extended well beyond that sliver of TSA membership and activity.

Hiding Dynamics at All Levels

As indicated above, among frontline employees, informal hiding attempts were rampant since reprimands generally resulted from being seen by management. But in addition to such behaviors among public-facing staff, hiding was perceived as a necessity throughout the organization, at almost all TSA hierarchical levels (including for managers) and in all activities (including formal ones). Almost no part of TSA therefore lent itself to being seen.

Hannah's inquisitive presence near checkpoints, then, was a paradigmatic example of the difficulties and opportunities of the interloper. Her presence was a bit like a combination of TSA staff's worst nightmare and an ideal opportunity to showcase their skills at remaining unseen.

First, screeners needed to hide the way they worked from outsiders. Screeners' formal expertise resided in their ability to detect hidden threats to the traveling public and to report them immediately. We learned later that, as part of ongoing quality control of their activities, managers would randomly flash fake x-ray images of prohibited items on x-ray operators' screens to test their detection abilities. (The x-ray machines are located near the security checkpoints, and a seated employee usually analyzes images of personal belongings brought on board.) The screeners operating the x-ray machines thus had to react constantly to hidden objects, and failure to do so could entail decertification from the job. The notion that anyone could hide something from screeners was therefore a constant source of concern.

At the same time, the efficacy of screeners' work hinged on the public not fully knowing how screening operated. This need to hide how TSA proceeded forced screeners to pay constant attention to "security sensitive information," or any information whose public release would be detrimental to transportation security. Each day, they were required to take many steps to safeguard such information by hiding it from outsiders.

Second, managers constantly feared—often for good reasons, given employees' behaviors—that something might be hidden from them. In a setting like TSA where leaders typically came from the ranks, these hiding dynamics inevitably percolated upwards in the hierarchy. Those promoted to leadership roles picked up on their staff's hiding attempts. On one hand, management occasionally detected and took offense at their employees' hiding practices. As supervisors observed about their team members, when they went somewhat out of sight on breaks or for lunch, they often took longer than expected. On the other hand, when trying to "keep an eye" on employees, several supervisors realized that it was difficult to keep track of them, even though they were working in plain sight.

A TSA supervisor detailed such a challenge and shared his trick for trying to notice people a bit more: "It's a blank [slate] to me, you know? So, I'll go out and [see] everybody's nametag, look at their nametag, and say their name a couple of times to them, you know, until it kind of sticks in there."

Getting to know one's staff was important not simply to oversee the team but also because the notion of internal missteps was often a cause for lingering anxiety among management. No supervisor wanted a security breach linked to an employee's misstep to occur under her or his watch.

When I had asked my seminar students to observe TSA operations (prior to the completion of the study referenced above), I had not anticipated this obsession with hiding as a form of field defense. In retrospect, I probably should have foreseen it, given the agency's security mission. Instead, I envisioned other potential defenses playing out and tried preemptively to defuse them, even though they ended up being quite irrelevant.

For instance, in one of the first meetings with TSA representatives about launching a research project, I brought up the fact that I was a dual Franco-American citizen and that I often worked with non-US doctoral students or research assistants.[15] I wanted to test any reservations TSA might have about involving noncitizens. Surprisingly, this disclosure triggered no red flags. Perhaps the simple fact of disclosing (regardless of contents disclosed) actually reassured TSA leaders that I was *not* hiding anything. But I did not yet pick up, at that time, the organization's main concern around (in)visibility. Rather, I recall thinking that the agency was quite welcoming and willing to engage with noncitizens: a testimony to the country's openness to engage with foreigners.

Another episode should have perhaps made me more attuned to visibility dynamics. Many screeners told us that every few months or so, they gathered to express their preferences in terms of gate assignments for the next period. It seemed a unique and strange ritual: the most senior employee would pick first, then the second most senior one, and so on, until the entire workforce had selected checkpoints. Some described it as being like a fraternity or sorority rush when friends call or text each other to know who got in and readjust their preferences based on others' placements. Despite our repeated requests to observe this matching process, it was deemed off-limits. "You cannot observe it," was the only answer we got. Once, however—late in our fieldwork and while interviewing an officer at the airport—a member of the research team noticed a commotion a few steps away. TSA officers were lining up, it seemed, to speak with what looked like a "suit" (i.e., someone who wore civilian clothes to work and therefore usually ranked higher in the hierarchy).

The interloper could not help but peek and realized that she was seeing the matching process; yet at the same time, she knew we had been told *not* to observe it. When I debriefed with her on what had happened that day, her most salient recollection centered not as much on what she saw but instead on the feeling of knowing she had briefly and inadvertently seen something off-limits. I, too, recall a thrill running through my body as she recounted that sighting. By *not* looking any longer, she felt she had done the right thing: a decision that likely also echoed what she perceived to be TSA's unease with being seen.

That peculiar exchange and the emotional reaction it triggered among us probably required way more probing than we both understood at the time. Only in retrospect did it gain in significance. We *ourselves* were starting to integrate TSA's taboo on not observing what should not be seen. In fact, it almost felt as if she were telling me an embarrassing secret when she recounted that fleeting episode.

Our unease around that moment should have raised more questions about the centrality of hiding in this specific setting.

One reason we did not focus on it for longer relates, in part, to the unique challenge interlopers face when dealing with such a defense mechanism.

Hiding's Implications for Interlopers

When properly implemented, hiding can offer a significant challenge to fieldworkers. It is a powerful field defense mechanism since the contentious topic (that requires hiding) never surfaces and does not receive any official recognition. Hiding's potency lies, in part, on our inability as interlopers to get a field member to admit that an issue is at stake. Unlike obstructing—which, as noted in the previous chapter, at least forces an up-front acknowledgment of an issue's existence—hiding never really calls for other field participants to "react" to something. Consequently, hiding provides few opportunities to get confirmation that an issue is unraveling.

Hiding from public view is also one of the most opaque defenses that fields can put forward. We cannot know what we don't see. It is only when hiding fails that what has been concealed is fully revealed, and only then must participants justify their past actions. After the revelation, interlopers can easily call a field or an organization to account. Still, prior to the revelation, a thick veil obscures the contentious activities. This veil requires no open discussion.

At the same time, hiding can backfire when interlopers start intuitively noticing absences, even though they might not yet realize that these absences are actively (whether intentionally or not) engineered.[16] Hence, hiding attempts can also be a chance for attentive interlopers to develop meaningful knowledge of a field.

After his visit to the Soviet Union, for example, the writer André Gide (1937) published a lambasting account of life in a country that he deemed too focused on egalitarianism. He had been invited by the Soviet government to tour several regions and was only shown what the regime favored. He could not help but notice, however, some oddities in available goods in shops and in the furnishing of dwellings. Moreover, he knew that "each of the Soviet states had once its popular art." So, given its absence from stores, Gide asked, "What has become of them?" Adding rhetorically, "Should it not be the work of an intelligent directing body to bring [them] back into use."[17] Also, when touring dwellings in a kolkhoz, he wrote about "the impression of complete depersonalization" conveyed by the same furniture and the same portrait of Stalin, but also by the absence of "smallest object" or "smallest personal souvenir."[18] What he did not see, but anticipated seeing, proved as powerful as what he was shown. The missing elements were, in part, what cued him to what might be hidden to his view.

What's hidden—or at least those that hide—can be the "absent presences" that "augment the power of the invisible," since their uncanny absence *underlines* what's missing.[19] Repeated absences and missing people can gradually attract attention if their presence is expected. As the sociologist Kathleen Blee explains, when she started studying women in the Ku Klux Klan, she realized that women constituted nearly half of the Klan membership in some US states. And yet, most accounts of the Klan portrayed "its terror through the images of bigoted, hate-filled white men, not women."[20] Where were the women? The Klan itself in its heyday only reluctantly acknowledged women's roles in its activities, since it viewed their political role as "both separate and subordinate to that of men."[21] Yet the repeated absence of women in the Klan's public representations directed Blee to probe into women's (little-known) political role. Hiding can sometimes be uncovered paradoxically because of its efficacy—when absent presences give preeminence to the concealed.

Another interloper, a Red Cross visitor to the Nazis' "model" concentration camp and ghetto Theresienstadt during World War II, also remarked on such absent presences. The Danish Red Cross representative visited it in 1943, right after Nazi "beautification" efforts, which were meant to hide their ongoing crimes. The extensive visit was a complete sham, carefully orchestrated by the Nazis to impress upon the outside world that the residents were well taken care of. The visitor seemed, however, puzzled by not being able to see the school and the maternity ward. He noticed the school building, but "unfortunately it was closed for 'vacation,' " he was told.[22] His report emphasized "that he had not seen any actual [operating] schools, but only one kindergarten." Similarly, he inquired about birthing facilities and was told the camp had some, but sadly "there was no opportunity to view [them]" at the time. We can only hypothesize how many more missing expected elements would have been necessary to uncover the true scale of the sham campaign and to convince this visitor to spell out in his final report what he suspected might be happening.

The stakes associated with every hiding attempt vary widely, of course, across fields. Being fired for misconduct at TSA pales in comparison to being marched to one's death at an extermination camp. From TSA to Theresienstadt, the range of field tensions that can be unearthed proves incommensurable. That said, every noticed hiding defense helps us better grasp what might be happening in each context.

For analytical clarity, I present and discuss in this book each defense mechanism (like hiding) in isolation from others. Yet the question of whether hiding and obstructing can go hand in hand and form cumulative defenses against interlopers is worth asking.

In any field, the mere fact of obstructing access already points to what might be hidden. Consequently, few fields couple the mechanisms of hiding and obstructing. From the interloper's vantage point, any obstruction, even though frustrating, constitutes a small win. It suggests that something troubles field participants and deserves more scrutiny. To keep something truly hidden, no one can mention even the impossibility of access: saying "no" to an inquiry into a given issue already reveals its existence.

Hence, interlopers are likely better off facing obstruction than encountering attempts at hiding. Instances of obstruction offer at least a tentative hold, whereas hiding provides interlopers little traction to pursue their quest.

With the benefit of hindsight, I cannot help but wonder whether Jack's welcoming posture and seeming absence of obstruction had not blinded me to some key dynamics at TSA. The welcoming impression I got from interacting with him never dampened throughout the many years the study lasted. He always tried his best to facilitate our research inquiry. I felt, in these moments, very lucky to be working with him. Jack seemed more like a cooperative ally than an intransigent gatekeeper. I went to him for answers, and he always seemed to deliver. His reassuring, burly, and smiling presence often encouraged me to continue when doubts on the direction of the study emerged.

Yet the apparent absence of any obstruction also probably led me slightly off course. For instance, only very late in the study's timeline did I hear rumors about the workplace being under court order to increase the representation of underrepresented minorities. The low number of Black and Latinx employees in the workforce was hard to miss, but I did not think twice about it at the time, guessing it was representative of the agency's historical formation. In addition, it took me a long time to locate a public governmental report on favoritism at TSA. In the local airport, such favoritism most likely would have involved promoting people coming from a specific group (such as the Coast Guard) over other employees, particularly to key positions at TSA. Jack himself, as I mentioned earlier, had come from the Coast Guard. The implications, however, of his prior employment record had not really registered as noteworthy during most of my time in the field.

Had we missed other "hidden" dynamics because we were rarely ever denied access? Might the possible reluctant disclosure of previously off-limits information have helped us better understand this context? Would a grumpy and obstructive Jack have been an asset rather than a hindrance to our inquiry?

Of course, I will never know the answers to the above questions. As field researchers and interlopers, we dream of field sites or organizations welcoming us warmly. It is much harder to imagine the "luck" we might have from seeing a door slammed in our face and from strongly suspecting that something is being hidden from us.

Should I thank Hannah's detainment or Jack's welcoming embrace for pushing me to examine more closely the visibility dynamics at TSA? I doubt the answer is as obvious as it might seem. Both surely played a role in the study's focus on hiding behaviors and their link to the rise of surveillance at work. Despite the frustration of encountering field defenses, we often forget that they reveal as much about a field as they protect it. Perhaps we should feel more appreciative next time a field participant tries to hide something from us or engage in other forms of resistance.

It would be a mistake nonetheless to depict interlopers as always holding the moral high ground—by revealing a hidden truth—and field participants as stuck in the low ground—by scheming to deceive. Interlopers are not immune to engaging in their own hiding games. Identifying these practices in ourselves is an essential step in building our ability to recognize such hiding in others.

For example: it is considered necessary, and even honorable, for fieldworkers to break down the use of hiding as a line of defense when met in the field. But at the same time, it is often seen as perfectly acceptable for *us* to hide some field features when, for instance, publishing our own findings. Anonymizing the towns or companies studied, using pseudonyms when quoting a person, and other hiding strategies: all these are part of the fieldworker's classic tool kit.[23] We generally claim to use these strategies to "protect" subjects in the field.

In many instances, we also try to "hide" ourselves from our fields because we believe certain disclosures might taint or endanger our access or data collection. TSA officers, therefore, are not the only ones trying to hide in plain sight.

Regarding TSA, I hid from my contacts there a key reason I got interested in their operations. Specifically, during a certain period (post-9/11), I was invariably selected and pulled out of large groups of travelers for added scrutiny when crossing US borders. My Middle Eastern background (on my father's side) might have triggered those supplementary inspections. Over time, I learned to shave my stubble before traveling (in the hope of avoiding being pulled aside); I instinctively did the same when going to conduct interviews or observations at TSA. Yet what we hide from others teaches us as much about them as about ourselves.

At the time I started studying airport security officers, the agency had issued an internal policy "requiring enhanced screening for persons from and traveling through thirteen Arab and Muslim countries and Cuba."[24] I was unaware of that policy. But I did pick up on the higher frequency with which I was being screened, compared, for instance, to my (fair-skinned) spouse, despite him being a non–US citizen. I did feel that hiding features that could (mis)identify me as possibly Arab or Muslim seemed to ease my passage through borders.

Such mimicking or countermimicking strategies of field behaviors offer indirect ways to surface the hidden and unknown. What I was attempting to hide in the field resonated with what the field was hiding from travelers (i.e., TSA's screening procedure) and partly mirrored a key field concern at the time around whom to screen to best protect travelers.

Every field researcher, I suspect, can recount a variant on this story: when their own behavior (such as hiding) mirrors a field's tension. The sociologist C. J. Pascoe's study of gender and sexuality among high school boys provides a fascinating example of these dynamics and what they can reveal about the setting she examined. When observing young men's behaviors in a high school, she decided to adopt a "least-gendered identity" to maintain a good relationship with the boys.[25] This meant hiding her female gendered identity as much as she could. Yet many students refused to let this cover-up fly: several boys propositioned her, regardless, as a potential sexual partner; other girls asked her probing questions, to see whether she was into girls or boys.[26] Pascoe nonetheless held firm; she "camped up" her sexuality and performed "what might be identified as a soft-butch lesbian demeanor": walking with a swagger in her shoulders rather than in her hips, and more.[27] She did this so consistently that by the end of the research, she frequently mimicked some of the boys' masculinizing strategies (often involving sexual innuendo) when interacting with them.

Another aspect of herself that Pascoe systematically tried to hide was her own sexuality. While the high school girls in the school's Gay/Straight Alliance had (rightly) a more secure sense that she was gay—and were fine with leaving it at that— some others felt they needed to probe more inquisitively. When cornered, her reply was that she could answer the question once her research project was completed. The decision to hide that she was living with a woman when conducting her research was motivated by her desire to connect and learn. Without such hiding on her part, Pascoe suggests, her strong rapport with the boys might have weakened, and she could not have documented the sexist and homophobic discourse that allowed them to uphold their masculine identities.

The exact elements that Pascoe opted to hide (gender and sexuality) ended up being at the core of her study's findings, since she documents how teenage boys repeatedly repudiate an image of failed masculinity to live up to their expected gendered and sexual identity. Like treasure-hunters unsure of what they are going after, interlopers often cannot fully articulate what might escape their gaze. Yet by hiding select parts of themselves in the field, they anticipate what they believe might "react" with the setting they are studying.

What would have happened had she passed instead as either a straight or gay woman? Would she have fit more easily into the gendered and sexual imagery upheld by the boys or been prevented from listening in on their conversations? Would coming out as gay not have hidden enough of herself, to the point of derailing her data collection? Conversely, would adopting a straight persona prove too deceptive? Similarly, would disclosing my experience of being screened frequently at US airports have derailed my study as well? And would pretending to be only a US citizen rather than a dual-national have been too misleading?

All these questions highlight how we regularly engage in intricate hiding dances in the field and how what we opt to hide can uncannily mirror what's most at stake for all. In these hiding reversals, we invariably develop an imagined relationship with the field and, at the same, time try to counter the symbiosis. The more we recognize our own hiding behavior, the easier it becomes to spot it in others as well.

CHAPTER THREE

Shelving

"WHY DON'T YOU JOIN our committee on organizational culture? You would be a great fit, given all that you've done." That request came from a senior colleague at the Harvard Business School while I was still on its faculty. The moment I was asked to join, I sensed my unease. By then, I had worked for several years on a research project on faculty socialization at the school (this will be described in more detail in the next chapter), and the question of moralizing business education had emerged as a dominant theme in my inquiry. My colleagues were aware of this induced focus. Also, this person and other close colleagues probably noticed I was starting to feel that the school's avowed higher moral goals did not always align with the practices I observed on the ground.

I felt very ambivalent about this request to join the committee, so I tried at first to decline. Up to then, I had been very careful in my ongoing study not to capture data that the school or the university might deem private (i.e., faculty meeting discussions and departmental hiring deliberations). I took every step I could to preserve this boundary and my academic freedom. I feared that joining the committee might put me in an awkward position. Joining might even constrain my future ability to publicly disseminate some of my study's findings. This new assignment would surely complicate my task.

More importantly, I also wasn't sure the school really wanted to change its culture. In this century-old institution with many defenders, the majority view seemed to be that the "brand" must remain strong.[1] Put another way: I knew there were legitimate concerns facing the school, and the committee's creation *seemed* to signal that the school took those concerns seriously. But what if the committee was instead a way to publicly appear to address criticism while quietly forestalling any change? Looking back, I didn't want to join, because I also didn't want to be taken on what I felt could be a useless ride.

Several days later, this same person approached me again to inquire about my decision. The idea underlying the creation of this new committee was to improve the school's culture, and my insights would be valued, I was told. Didn't I have a unique perspective on its inner workings? I could see the point but tried again to maneuver out of it. I would think about it, I replied, and offered to consult with other senior colleagues before providing a final answer. They strongly encouraged me to join; one even argued that the committee lacked sexual minority representation, perhaps to shame me even more into agreeing to participate.[2] Despite my mixed feelings, I reluctantly accepted. Luckily, the committee did not meet too often or for too long. I was relieved once my service on it ended but also felt that I had just avoided a landmine.

Nearly a decade later, I probed into a case that will be detailed in this chapter: puppeteers employed by Disneyland Resort who tried to unionize but were then left in limbo by Disney, despite their employer's apparent efforts to accommodate their needs. It was only by studying the Disney puppeteers' story that I realized I had probably come very close to seeing my concerns being "shelved" in that HBS committee. The Harvard Business School, as an institution, was acknowledging the need to examine its own culture, deploying efforts to seemingly address issues that might be linked to it. And yet, at the same time, the institution did not really seem to want to change.[3] This shelving, whether done consciously or not, provided a way for the school to defend itself against interlopers probing into its unique culture.

It's rare to read comprehensive accounts of the shelving of an interloper's inquiry. Many of us likely experience fleeting episodes of shelving, or periods when we sense that, despite surface efforts to advance an issue, field contacts seem really to want to stall it indefinitely. But we then find other ways to reengage with our field or shift settings and tend not to remain frozen in place.

Still, there are, to my knowledge, no scholars that have reported in-depth on research quests that never succeeded *because* they got shelved. Indeed, there is little to write about, and there are even fewer "findings" to show. The anthropologist Laura Bohannan's brilliant "fictional" account of her difficulties accessing the African tribe she finally studied—a book not only subtitled "An Anthropological Novel" but also initially published under a pen name—points to the strong institutional barriers to disclosing even partial disappointments.[4] One would expect that apparent "complete failures" to access a site would be even harder to find in print. Predictably, I could not locate a detailed academic account of shelving.

That's why this chapter deliberately highlights an example not from academia but instead from labor organizers, so as to illuminate this hard-to-document yet critical field defense mechanism. Regrettably, the case of the Disneyland Resort puppeteers captures such a shelving well. The puppeteers aspired to something different, responded to Disney's perceived attempt to change their working conditions, and ultimately were left with little to show for it. Unlike other chapters, this one is less ethnographic in nature, since I report other people's attempts at accessing a field. As I see it, the benefits of spotlighting and importing such a defense mechanism into fieldworkers' broader tool kit of known defenses outweighs this potential limitation.

Nearly two years had gone by since Disney was first officially notified that its puppeteers—specifically, those working on the *Disney Junior—Live on Stage!* show at the Disney California Adventure Park—had filed for union representation.[5] Now, on March 31, 2017, a new labor contract was finally agreed upon. Moreover, a few puppeteers even received back pay from a settlement in mid-February 2017, just weeks before the ratification. A deal and some apparent closure had at last been reached. Yes, it was true that by the end of labor negotiations, nearly half of the initial puppeteers who had been working on the show were no longer employed at Disneyland due to exhaustion or the pursuit of alternative employment. Even so, March 31 still felt like a big victory and a vindication of all the hours spent organizing. Disney had agreed in principle to a labor contract specific to puppeteers.

But only a few days later, on April 9, 2017, the show that employed these remaining and soon to be unionized puppeteers abruptly closed. The victory was therefore bittersweet. Before that spring, the *Disney Junior—Live on Stage!* show had employed close to thirty puppeteers, performing roles such as Mickey Mouse, Donald Duck, and Goofy. In April, most of the puppeteers lost their jobs. A few continued working after the closure, but they did so in less desirable positions that did not utilize their unique skills. (These positions were mostly entry-level ones that required walking and parading in the park but did not entail puppet manipulation.) A contract for puppeteers was now on the Disney books. And yet, no puppeteer performing at the Disneyland Resort was covered by it.

Three years prior to the closure, the majority of puppeteers working on the show voted to join the American Guild of Variety Artists (AGVA) labor union. They did so to demand better working conditions and wages. As reported in the press at the time, "soon after [the organizing drive], the guild filed an unfair labor practice complaint with the National Labor Relations Board, alleging that year [2015] that Disney reduced their work hours and took other retaliatory actions."[6] The guild also filed that same year a second complaint, on the definition and classification of the puppet specialist position in the Disneyland Resort's nomenclature. The union's complaints about puppeteers' labor concerns were combined and settled in December 2015, with Disney offering "the puppeteers about $167,000 in back pay."[7] (This was the money they finally got in 2017, before the new contract was agreed upon.)

The 2015 settlement did not, however, address a key issue at stake for most puppeteers. That is, it did not recognize their work as expert performers (akin to actors), rather than merely unskilled, underpaid employees. When the union offered in 2015 to fold puppeteers into the same contract it had negotiated for other live performers at the Disneyland Resort, the company declined. Instead, it opted to discuss a new contract with AGVA that would be specific to puppeteers. After the NLRB settlement was reached,[8] a tentative new contract covering puppeteers was finalized. This led some puppeteers to take "solace" in the fact that even if they departed from Disney, "a contract could apply to future puppeteers who want to work at the resort."[9] But that potential success proved elusive.

To date, no puppeteers have been hired under this 2017 labor contract, which in fact expired in 2020. As for the handful of puppeteers still working there, they have returned to what they describe mockingly as "talking head" roles that merely roam the park. As one puppeteer retrospectively notes, the entire process "made me understand that they [Disney] did not care that I was a skilled worker."[10] Not only do these remaining puppeteers not have jobs as puppeteers, then, the jobs they do have do not fall under the new contract for which they fought.

These puppeteers organized for better working conditions and higher pay, and they did succeed in securing back pay and temporary workplace accommodations (e.g., "allotted 20 minutes each day to work out in a training room to prepare for the rigors of the show"). Yet this victory occurred only after lengthy labor negotiations; and it was these drawn-out negotiations that ultimately allowed Disney to *shelve* the topic of recognizing puppeteers' unique skills.

Put another way, Disney de facto relegated to an indefinite future time the question of recognizing puppeteers' skills. As with my fears regarding the HBS committee, Disney acknowledged the issue of recognition when engaging with interlopers, and even deployed efforts to seemingly address it.[11] But actually, such acknowledgment only ensured that little progress ensued: the exact definition of shelving.

To better understand this shelving process—as well as why enacting a labor contract between Disney and its puppeteers would have proved a landmark advancement for the puppetry world—requires contextualizing puppeteers' often tense relations with their employers. What puppeteers and their union representatives were fighting for was more than better wages and more preparation time before performing their acts. They were fighting for recognition of their craft and for improved safety on the job.

In this specific case, the interlopers were the puppeteers who wished to unionize, but the dynamics described apply, more broadly, to any interlopers (including fieldworkers) being shelved. Shelving entails not only a unique form of field defense, but also one that is uniquely suited to the Disney context in which maintaining the appearances of carefully listening to and being highly reactive to constituents' needs (such as customers' and employees' demands) is core to field participants' organizational culture and decision-making process. Keeping everyone seemingly happy is a foundation of Disney's "smile factory" and worldview.[12]

Puppeteers and Their Employers: An Often Tense Relationship

Puppeteers have long had frequently contentious relationships with their patrons and employers, particularly with respect to the degree of ownership of and artistic control over the characters they perform. More generally, these conflicts also implicitly touch on employers' willingness to recognize the kind of work that puppeteers engage in. While employers like to see puppeteers as inexperienced hired hands, puppeteers view themselves as a highly skilled workforce based on the years of training required to master their craft.

Ever since the sixteenth century when traveling puppeteers brought shows to towns and gathered audiences in public spaces, local authorities have tried to control their work.[13] Whether for political or financial reasons, puppeteers' independence did not generally sit well with established orders. For many puppeteers, fines, summons, and expulsions were the norm. Even when tolerated or hired, their actions were restricted, as evidenced by countless regulations enacted across geographies.

Still today, in New York City's Central Park, for instance, authorities retaliate against puppeteers if caught performing in nondesignated spots.[14] Also, in the town of Hickory, North Carolina, puppeteers are barred from obstructing sidewalks and cannot violate "the prohibitions on disturbing, annoying and unnecessary noise."[15] Similarly, on boardwalks of summer resorts like Ocean City, puppeteers and other street performers are asked to register for and only perform in designated areas or face fines.[16] And when they are occasionally hired by local authorities to entertain audiences, their employers insist that puppeteers not solicit additional donations while performing.[17]

This desire to control puppeteers' behavior probably traces its roots to associations between puppetry and protest. From giant puppets seen in street parades during the Great Depression to those manipulated by the militant Bread and Puppet Theater in the 1960s, puppets' political and satirical messages are often intrinsic to the craft and hard to ignore.[18] Even today, at least one state (New York) reserves itself the right to decide who can be deemed and hired as a puppeteer, and court rulings have at times described some puppeteers as "protestors."[19] In short, state authorities (and most employers) remain suspicious of puppeteers' unchecked behavior.[20]

But despite the long-standing controls imposed on puppeteers, it is only recently that control has been sought over puppeteers' characters (namely, the final result of puppeteers' work). In the last decades, attempts to appropriate characters have become more common. In a landmark 1977 case, puppeteers Sid and Marty Krofft—who developed the characters Pufnstuf and Mayor McCheese for a children's television show—obtained significant damages from the McDonald's Corporation after it started using very similar characters in commercials without their consent.[21] That ruling suggested that puppeteers owned the characters they had developed thanks to their unique skills.

Again, now in the 1990s, a coffee manufacturer tried to gain control of two characters that Jim Henson and his colleagues had performed in this company's commercials.[22] The court similarly sided with the puppeteers, noting that "it was not customary for puppeteers to part with all rights in their puppets in the 1950s and 1960s [when the characters were developed] because puppeteers generally continue to and expect to perform their puppets in subsequent performances."[23] Here, the court found that in light of his practice and the nature of Jim Henson's art form, "he would not have intended, and did not intend, to transfer rights to his puppets in perpetuity or to separate himself from their performances and creative control over them."[24]

Recently, there has been a rise in screen work available to puppeteers in addition to, or instead of, stage work for puppeteers, alongside the consolidation of media companies and employers.[25] Consequently, fresh debates have arisen over the question of whether puppeteers have a say in the puppets and characters they perform and, indirectly, whether they are skilled artists and creators or mere hired hands and operators. A 2001 court ruling, for instance, on the Howdy Doody puppet's ownership crystallized these growing tensions by acknowledging puppeteers' right to own their puppets. After Howdy Doody's main puppeteer's death, the court noted that when the television show went off the air, "Rufus Rose [its puppeteer] ended his employment by NBC but kept possession of many of the puppets used in the show."[26] Puppeteers' rights as artists and creators seemed affirmed.

But gradually, caveats have been raised and practices have shifted slightly. As an example of this shift, in 2017—the same year that Disneyland Resort closed the live show employing puppeteers—its parent company also fired another puppeteer: Steve Whitmire, the person who had voiced Kermit the Frog for twenty-seven years. Despite Whitmire's desire to continue performing the character and a statement that he "would never consider abandoning Kermit," he was forced out of his puppet.[27] This happened after the Muppets (including its Kermit character) joined the Disney portfolio in 2004, and Disney executives started taking a more active role in production and artistic decisions.

Such an exercise of control became evident when Disney asked puppeteer Matt Vogel to replace Whitmire as the Kermit the Frog puppeteer. The reason Disney gave for replacing Whitmire was his "repeated unacceptable business conduct over a period of many years."[28] But according to him, it was his being "outspoken on character issues"[29] and "speaking out about changes to Kermit" that landed him in trouble.[30]

Regardless of the reasons, the firing of Whitmire made evident that, under certain circumstances, puppeteers did not control characters they had long performed. Moreover, they were seen, at least by Disney, as more like hired hands than artists. And this was the precise issue—recognizing puppeteers' unique skills and roles—that Disneyland Resort was apparently trying to shelve.

Puppeteers' Working Conditions at the Disneyland Resort

Staging and performing live shows four to six times per day at the Disney California Adventure Park might sound like fun, but for puppeteers, it was a physically taxing activity. They needed to keep one hand in the air for more than twenty minutes per show while also "rolling around from one side to the other fast" (in the words of one puppeteer) and manipulating other parts of the puppet. Over time, the puppets became increasingly heavy and uncomfortable, meaning that puppeteers needed to train a lot more to perform their characters well and remain strong enough to endure the whole day.

These heavier puppets were built by a shop less attuned to the strenuousness of the job, gradually replacing the lighter ones initially built by the Jim Henson Company. The new puppets, one puppeteer recalled, were "heavier and made out of two-inch-thick foam rubber, not built for the human body, especially not in those positions." Athletic trainers were provided by Disney to develop strength programs for puppeteers. Still, the combination of overexertion and less than adequate puppet design resulted in many of them dealing with multiple injuries and physical therapy sessions.

With added rehearsals, breaks, and lunch periods, the official eight-hour day proved to be a grueling marathon for puppeteers. But despite the pain and bruises, they felt a sense of pride. As one of these puppeteers explains, "We were proud of what we did," and continuously wanted "to hone our craft." A shared sense of higher purpose motivated them: "We only wanted to work on ourselves to make a better show."

That pride, however, proved hard to sustain when Disney continued to treat them as unskilled labor despite their years on the job. In one puppeteer's recollection, Disney tried to portray the puppeteers' jobs as "teenager summer jobs" and repeatedly told them that their jobs were "not that important." When the puppeteers started to express a desire to unionize, Disney representatives encouraged them "not to care as much about" what they were doing.

In 2015, among the puppeteers working in live stage shows at the Disneyland Resort, several had worked for almost ten years on these shows. Most initially joined Disney in entry-level jobs and only later auditioned to manipulate puppets.

Even so, these individuals received extensive training over the years by expert puppeteers to hone their needed skills. By the time of the unionization drive, several were now teaching new-comers how to manipulate the puppets and had become expert performers in their own right.

One reason for organizing was the level of pay, but it was also because of the continuous physical strain from the job.[31] Moreover, puppeteers deemed the day's breaks—two fifteen-minute breaks each day, as well as one thirty-minute break for lunch—to be insufficient to recuperate physically. During the show, they were on a stool, leaning over, with their heads under the stage, and often rolling in various positions. Head injuries were common. "We are hurt, we are breaking," recalled one performer. Another concurred, "There was a lot of pain . . . shoulders, back, pain from repetition and injuries from that." A third added that several performers had gone to the hospital for surgeries, including for a hernia and a back fracture.

The combination of low pay and hardship was difficult to reconcile with the level of mastery they had gradually reached at manipulating puppets, skillfully juggling characters and shows. "The expectations for us were higher than what we were being compensated [for] and how we were being treated. . . . We were still being treated as though we were just like little pawns or minions. To be told what to do as opposed to [being recognized as] the actual skilled people we had become," remembers one puppeteer. They therefore decided to explain to managers why they "thought they were skilled performers."

Their disgruntlement was further exacerbated by comparing themselves to the few "human liaisons" (namely, unionized live performers, who introduced and interacted with puppets on stage) that also participated in the shows. The tasks required of these performers seemed relatively less demanding than what puppeteers were asked to do. And yet live performers earned significantly more than them and had much more advantageous working conditions (e.g., a longer lunch break).

The unionizing drive, which officially commenced in November 2014, was a way for puppeteers to collectively voice their desire for more recognition. The decision to join a union was not an easy one. But ultimately the decision felt right to many of them because they wanted to work with puppets causing fewer injuries. As one explained, "We didn't have a voice and they [literally] didn't have our backs. I didn't want any longer to get hurt." There were a few hiccups (one-on-one managerial meetings; posters in break rooms discouraging employees from unionizing; removal of the puppeteers from shifts in other Park jobs) that resulted in unfair labor practice complaints and the National Labor Relations Board's involvement. Still, the puppeteers voted to be represented by a union.

The Shelving of Disney Puppeteers' Labor Concerns

Following the vote, Disney's HR representatives came to the table and decided to negotiate with the union on a new contract for puppeteers. The hope of a better future energized the puppeteers. Unfortunately, that negotiation dragged on for about two years, and the time involved was significant. One puppeteer noted in retrospect that "it was *not* a negotiation, it was them [Disney] making a power play." In particular, "the mistreatment of our time was the big one," since the meetings occurred one or two days per month, when the company could meet, and on employees' days off.

While a draft labor agreement finally emerged from these discussions, its making proved painful. Seeing their time disrespected, puppeteers spoke of the overall experience as "traumatic" and "disheartening." They described the strong emotions that gripped them while simultaneously explaining their love of the job alongside the medical expenses they incurred and their difficult living conditions. Many puppeteers had worked on Broadway or for renowned entertainment companies. Despite this experience, most were still offered very low wages at Disney, resulting in some living in their cars and requiring food stamps to eat.[32] Some of the puppeteers involved found that their "sense of worth went down the drain" and reported lasting self-questioning of their value.

Even if the company did not mean for the process to be antagonizing or demeaning, many puppeteers viewed it as such. For example, in the talks, Disney representatives told them that anybody could do the job, underscoring the puppeteers' perceived lack of necessary skills. One puppeteer recalls that the hardest part was "to sit across the table from managers and higher ups who [told you] your job has never meant anything and will never mean anything."

In an effort to dispute the skilled nature of puppeteers' work, Disney representatives attempted to demonstrate the purported ease in performing with the puppets in the designated spaces. A Disney representative held the standard Mickey puppet on their arm, while the puppeteers described the required movements. Due to the weight of the puppet and the amount of physical exertion, the person could not sustain their position for more than fifteen seconds. Puppeteers also recount instances in which Disney representatives were asked to demonstrate lip-synch movements, to no avail. Ultimately, however, these "skill tests" proved futile at convincing the company of the expertise required for the job.

Despite the proven difficulty of the puppeteers' jobs, Disney negotiators reasserted their stance that puppeteers were not deserving of equal pay like their more "highly skilled" performing counterparts (i.e., human stage actors and narrators). Company executives continued to "try and label people as much as possible as unskilled workers because they don't need to pay them as much." What angered puppeteers most was that "they [Disney] were willing to honor their dancers and singers [with union contracts], [but] they didn't want to honor their specialist performers. It was offensive, insulting," recalls a participant. Ultimately, one puppeteer confessed, "We want to make magic. We loved working at Disney. We hated working for the Disney Corporation." Another one summarized his feelings by noting, "I now have a love/hate relationship with Disney," because he loved the job but felt as if it was "an abusive relationship."

Critically, even today, the draft labor agreement has never been enacted, since the Disneyland Resort has not hired a single puppeteer under this new contract. The contract expired in April 2020, in part nullifying puppeteers' efforts to create better conditions for future hires. Several puppeteers suspected that the shelving was long planned. As one noted, "Disney management is amazing to seem like they want to fix your problems. It seems they were trained to make you feel better, like a therapist . . . But we wanted it fixed . . . and Disney is good at doing nothing!" Another puppeteer echoed this view that the non-outcome was engineered: there "was very much the attitude of 'no, this problem doesn't exist. This is not a problem. You're making it up. You should be fine. There's not an issue.'" With the labor issue now shelved, the show could go on. At least, that is, other Disney shows *without* puppeteers.

The above shelving example is particularly poignant because the Disneyland Resort puppeteers voiced hope until the end that the energy they deployed and the sacrifices they made would not be in vain. "We felt we needed to power through for the betterment of somebody at some point; we felt we had to push forward and fight the fight," recalled one participant. Another one echoed this viewpoint: "I have no regrets; we did this for the future generations of puppeteers. So that all new entrants don't immediately get injured." That said, the reality—that a legal framework to hire puppeteers was now set up but unfortunately not enacted for lack of hiring—left a bitter taste for those who fought for it.

Granted, some received back pay, and those sums are not negligible in light of puppeteers' precarious labor market. Yet overall, the extended timeline of negotiations and the relatively tenuous outcome explain why many puppeteers believe that this problem still does "not exist" from Disney's perspective. Like other interlopers hoping for access or a desired outcome, many of these puppeteers had imagined a path forward. Disney representatives' portrayal of a light at the end of the tunnel is what kept these interlopers going. The highs and lows only seemed like natural steps in the process.

One cannot help but suspect that the shelving might be a typical defense mechanism—possibly even used repeatedly by Disney executives—to guard against the unwanted attention drawn by these and other labor issues.[33] When a field is particularly keen on managing its image, shelving is an ideal defense mechanism, since it gives the impression that participants want to address an issue, while ensuring no action is really taken. Shelving is therefore more indicative of a field's main tension (here, the need to seem attentive and responsive to employees' concerns) than a reaction to interlopers' behavior. The more responsive or accountable a field is supposed to look, the more shelving is likely to occur.

Shelving is not unique to the Walt Disney Company. Many other organizations, including government agencies that launch public inquiries, have long adopted a similar line of defense. Taking as examples, among others, the 2003 Canadian Severe Acute Respiratory Syndrome Commission and the

2009 Australian Victorian Bushfires Royal Commission, the political scientist Alastair Stark notes in an article on shelving in politics that the idea of inquiries being used as management tools goes back to the early twentieth century. Central to this claim is that inquiries are "a means of defusing threatening issues" rather than actually solving them.[34]

Indeed, close observers of governmental politics described this idea of defusing tensions via shelving as early as 1937. As Hugh Clokie and Joseph Robinson explained, "when certain social groups, economic interests, or powerful sections of the community are aroused upon some question ... the Government has no alternative but to appoint a Commission of Inquiry. [Its] intentions may vary from a serious desire to get at the bottom of a topic ... to the other extreme of hoping to 'shelve' the question by apparently conciliatory actions which will provide indefinite postponement."[35]

Today, large private organizations also rely on shelving to diffuse troubling issues. I suspect that fields and organizations that rely heavily on shelving as a form of defense against interlopers are the ones most concerned, like Disney, with managing impressions. With large US corporations gradually backing away from their previous "social compact" with their employees yet still concerned about their "corporate social responsibility" image, shelving is an increasingly fitting defense.[36] More broadly, shelving remains a powerful and attractive defense mechanism for any field highly dependent on its external environment and needing to navigate competing demands.[37]

Shelving's Implications for Interlopers

Shelving carries many key implications for interlopers. But the first and perhaps most important one is that shelving forces interlopers to continuously assess and reassess the authenticity of field participants' intent. The line between believing and second-guessing participants is always shifting, forcing inter-lopers to doubt their own read of the situation. For them, deciphering any given action as a signal of progress or shelving proves very difficult.

For example, it is very difficult to establish that Disney executives and their HR professionals did *not* enter the above negotiations in good faith, and they might have truly wanted to hire puppeteers under this new AGVA contract to work in the Disneyland Resort. Under these circumstances, Disney did initially seem quite responsive to puppeteers' concerns and desire to find a resolution. That said, only the hiring of pup-peteers under the new contract would have really signaled that the company did *not* want to shelve the topic. Because this did not happen, one puppeteer aptly described the entire negotia-tion process as being "simply for show" and in no way a genu-ine effort on Disney's part.

A second and related key implication of shelving is the difficulty for interlopers to initially realize that their issue has been set aside and is no longer active. In the flurry of activities that predate the actual (final) shelving, a flicker of hope that a good outcome is within reach always seems to shine. Why would people come to the table and spend time on an issue if they did not want to see a resolution? Even when everything points to indefinite postponement, inter-lopers can still convince themselves that their efforts were worthwhile. The "solace" that the Disney puppeteers took in the idea that a contract could still apply to future hires underlines how such hopes persist.[38] The belief that unshelving is just around the corner—and that the next administration, leader, or generation of members will pick up where past par-ticipants left off—allows many labor organizers to continue their work.

Finally, the fact of *almost* being heard can itself prove to be a form of success for certain interlopers. As several puppeteers told us, the time they spent trying to iron out a contract felt like "the most validating professional" experience in their careers. Publicly voicing concerns in itself carries benefits, regardless of outcomes. It was through this process that they finally realized how unappreciated their skills were at the company and what they might be worth elsewhere.

Yet when faced with repeated shelving, interlopers who initially feel empowered can also easily burn out. Indeed, shelving hinges on people's limited attention span. The assumption is that by the time efforts to shelve are fully deployed, any given issue's key participants (including main protagonists, labor organizers, and field researchers) will have moved on to another issue or lost their interest, patience, or ability to voice their opinion. Here, the fact that many of the Disney puppeteers seeking recognition might no longer be working at the Resort a few years after unionizing facilitated this bet. Those most involved could no longer push its implementation, since many would no longer be present. Moreover, the few remaining ones did not have enough followers to continue advocating for their demands.

While it's inspiring to believe that a new cohort of individuals will take up the fight, the frequency with which a given field shelves issues is probably a better indicator of what's to come. In the same way that select British parliamentarians had the reputation of enthusiastically appointing endless commissions to infinitely stall any issue that came their way, some settings are known to bury issues by shelving them.[39] Their leaders can learn and reuse the craft that goes into defending themselves: by acknowledging an issue, deploying efforts seemingly to address it, and making sure no action ensues.

Under Emmanuel Macron's presidency, for example, the French government started repeatedly spearheading what it labeled "citizens' conventions" (*consultations citoyennes* in French); the European Union itself then promoted such processes. Within years, many pointed out that these governmental bodies rarely followed up on or implemented their recommendations. While observers noted the benefit of building citizens' involvement in public affairs, they also warned, "EU leaders [presumably including Macron] must now ensure that those who participated feel that their contributions have been heard. If this does not happen . . . citizens will feel that their contribution was meaningless."[40] Participation dies down when voices are not heard. This also explains why repeated shelving and interloper burnout can easily go hand in hand.

As I indicated in the chapter's opening, the implications for interlopers I spelled out above come not only from the Disneyland Resort case but also in part from my own experience of being nominated for a committee tasked with investigating HBS's culture. Upon reading, years later, Disney's response to the concerns of puppeteers at the Resort, this episode of near-shelving at HBS made me feel a kinship of sort with the puppeteers. At the time, the event had not coded in my mind as a typical form of field defense, because the silencing (discussed in the next chapter) was much louder. The school, however, was also very careful about managing its image, both internally and externally, and adept (like many other universities dependent on alumni donations) at forming ad hoc committees to explore—and sometimes shelve—any concerning issues.[41]

The combination of hope and, ultimately, frustration inherent in any shelving process—which I personally felt while on the culture committee—echoed how Disney puppeteers described their experience during and after the labor negotiations. Their shelving was, without doubt, much more comprehensive and consequential than mine. Losing one's ability to perform fulfilling work and earn a living from doing so can prove highly distressing. Still, the sense of being taking on a ride yet still hoping for a positive outcome is a common feeling for "shelved" interlopers, regardless of their circumstances. I suspect many readers can come up with their own episodes of shelving, whether in their institutions or in the field.

Interlopers know change is elusive, yet still dream it is within reach. The ride itself is often quite informative, as it captures a field's core cultural tenet and tension: in the Disney case, a desire to keep park employees "smiling" while also adamantly denying them the skill-recognition they felt they deserved. This desire to appear concerned with an issue, while simultaneously not wanting to take any action, is a tension likely present in this and other settings. Instances of shelving therefore teach us not only about interlopers' specific concerns but also about other field participants' collective projected desires.

CHAPTER FOUR

Silencing

SNOW HAD ALREADY started falling on the ground. Looking out the window from her faculty office at the Harvard Business School, Carol could see tall trees speckling the landscaped campus. The trees' powdery white coats offered a beautiful contrast to the redbrick buildings. As always, the view looked enchanting. It did not distract her, however, from the tasks ahead. She had class sessions to organize and new teaching materials to absorb.[1] Leading class sessions was almost a sacred pursuit within the school walls. The time spent preparing to ensure that all would go smoothly in the classroom occupied much of faculty members' time during teaching semesters.

Carol was no exception, but the ringing office phone interrupted her as she was finalizing her teaching plan. The National Weather Service had issued a winter storm warning that morning, and she knew that the other faculties of Harvard University—that is, those *not* teaching at HBS—were slowly canceling classes across campuses. An HBS program administrator greeted her when she answered the call and told her that the Dean's office was monitoring the situation. She wanted nonetheless to inquire about Carol's plans.[2]

The request confused Carol a bit, since HBS prided itself in never closing its classrooms. Even when Harvard College announced a snow day, the business school tended to remain open. The idea of sending (high-paying) executive education participants back home or asking first-year MBA students to remain in their on-site dormitory rooms because of snow rarely crossed anyone's mind at the school. In addition, during the student protests of the late 1960s, HBS—unlike other parts of the university—continued to function, as the *Harvard Crimson* student newspaper put it, "normally."[3] Be it snow, social unrest, or any other impediments, the expectation was for all hands on deck at HBS.[4] With all these elements in mind, Carol wondered why anyone was asking about her teaching plans.

"It's up to you to decide," the person calling her told her. She was simply making the rounds of faculty members scheduled to teach the next day and checking with them to see whether they needed to make alternate plans. "Is anyone else canceling classes?" probed Carol. Not to the caller's knowledge, but again she reassured Carol that she should do what *she* felt was right. "It is entirely up to you to make the call," the administrator repeated, assuring her that "we will support you either way." A long silence followed. In that moment, she realized what was being asked of her. She needed to "decide"—perhaps for the record—that she would hold her classes.

Despite all Carol knew about HBS's history of never canceling classes, it seemed important to the caller that she "make" the decision and that the administration not be seen as imposing a course of action upon its faculty members. "Yes, of course, I will be holding class," Carol replied. "Good," chimed in the caller, now suddenly perkier. She then thanked Carol and hung up. Carol had made the "right" call. Importantly, she did so of her own volition and without seemingly being forced to teach despite the upcoming snowstorm.

Silence can generally seem soothing. In other instances, however, silence can be deafening.⁵ In HBS's context, more than a century of fine-tuning the school's culture has imbued silence with much louder meaning than it might appear.⁶ The above exchange between Carol and the caller reads as anodyne, almost anecdotal to a casual observer. Yet it also signals how field participants can engineer and manipulate silence in the pursuit of normative goals. The caller was experienced enough to know what *not* to do (i.e., tell a faculty member that she had to teach during a snowstorm), and Carol was seasoned enough to know how to react to the inquiry (i.e., clearly signaling that she had *independently* opted to hold classes). The combination of an apparent absence of coercion and a resulting proper outcome made for the perfect HBS moment.

Society—when at the level of small groups, and when left to its own device—"has always been able to cohere," wrote the Harvard sociologist George Homans.⁷ The caller's silence on articulating good behavior was instrumental in allowing Carol to do the right thing and to help this specific group cohere. The back-and-forth between silence and normative aspirations is a craft that HBS faculty members have long honed, one that I stumbled into somewhat unknowingly as an HBS junior faculty. Carol's moment of coherence illustrates how fields and organizations might favor silence when dealing with interlopers, both as a way to "educate" them on making proper calls and to quash any deviant's behavior.

Before discussing in more depth how this silence operated at HBS, I will detail why the school's handling of moral issues is a perfect example of this unique form of field defense. By silencing, I mean "the social construction of a space in which and about which subjects and words normally used in everyday life are not spoken."⁸ While silencing exists in many contexts, it is particularly salient in the one described in this chapter. Notably, this silencing defense was entirely in character with the field's core belief about how morality should be manufactured.

Like many older elite institutions that have relied historically on gentlemen's agreements to operate, HBS has long embraced an unspoken code of conduct. Unlike others, however, it also went to great lengths to engineer its day-to-day activities to ensure that any new member strictly obeys it. Because a key part of this code entails promoting moral relativism (i.e., the belief that each individual call is the right one), individual faculty members are strongly encouraged *not* to forcefully voice moral opinions that they believe apply to *all* members of the collective. Instead, everyone should "freely" decide for themselves. Silencing is the mechanism that enables such moral relativism.

Harvard Business School might seem like a strange setting to discuss higher moral aims, but such moral considerations have long permeated elite US business schools.[9] If technical skills alone were at stake, a vocational school could (and, historically, did) easily supplant today's elite business schools. In fact, the skill set taught in many high-ranked US business schools would be notably limited, were it not for its social component: namely, the development of soft skills and a social network, but also the learning of proper business conduct.

Such a view was embraced by HBS's first dean, who defined business as the "activity of making things to sell at a profit— decently."[10] The use of the term "decently" underlined his hope for developing a heightened sense of responsibility among students. Likewise, HBS's first great benefactor, George F. Baker, president of the First National Bank, was also quite explicit about his goal. "My life has been given to business," Baker explained in 1924, "and I should like to found the first Graduate

School to give a new start to better business standards."[11] Regardless of actual outcomes, the stated desire for higher goals was still very much part of HBS's DNA when I joined the school as an assistant professor in 2005, right out of my doctoral studies.

At first, when I signed on as a faculty member at HBS, I was entirely unaware of this moral goal. It took me time to decipher the school's agenda. I do recall hesitating once I received the HBS job offer, perhaps because I sensed a strong normative bent at the school. As a youth having had to occasionally face fairly unwelcoming cultures, I already knew of my potential familiarity yet unease with normative controls.[12] That said, I did not imagine a school—especially one part of a larger university with a lofty motto like *Veritas*—aiming for anything but traditional academic knowledge creation and dissemination.

Quickly after my arrival, however, new attention to the corporate morals—or lack thereof—at the school was ignited with the 2007 Enron energy company accounting scandal and the revelation that its CEOs trained at HBS. By 2008, the Lehman Brothers involvement in the subprime mortgage crisis and subsequent bankruptcy further raised scrutiny of businesses' moral responsibilities and, implicitly, of the role played by their leaders' training grounds in these dubious moral outcomes.

These events coincided with my decision to explore a study of HBS's faculty socialization efforts. Unsurprisingly, the historical moral undertones still seemed central to a lot of the onboarding I noticed and personally experienced as faculty at the school. The conflation of my lived experience and external events made a study of the school's moral backbone feel timely and needed. Still, how the school went about promoting a moral agenda seemed less clear to me. This was why I decided to dig deeper into those dynamics. Little did I know that the answer to this moral conundrum would be silence.

To learn more about the school, in 2008 I started seriously digging into the HBS archives. I knew I was walking a tight-rope, because others who had investigated the school's inner workings—and reported critically on it—had been the targets of the institutional gatekeepers' recent and full wrath. The journalist Brigid Sweeney wrote a 2008 piece in *Boston Maga-zine* about the school's partying culture, which led the school to voice its anger, as well as its feeling of being deceived.[13] A senior HBS staff informed everyone by email about the pub-lication and the school's response: "We have every right to feel deceived and angry about the final article. However, attempt-ing to refute hearsay and third-party accounts is typically ineffective." Instead, a pointed conversation with the publisher about the misleading and inappropriate actions of the writer would occur. Shortly after, when the journalist Philip Broughton published his 2009 insider account of student life at the school, the reaction was similarly forceful.[14] We learned that a communications plan to proactively counteract what the school felt were the most significant misstatements was set in motion.

Thus, it is not as if I did not know that I might be engaging in a potential acrobatic balancing act by pursuing my inquiry into the school's inner workings. But my curiosity about living in what felt like an exotic field nonetheless pushed me forward. I submitted application materials for the proposed study design to Harvard University's Institutional Review Board and soon got approved.

HBS's Moral Relativism and Silence

After receiving approval to proceed with the study, I tried a variety of approaches to collect and analyze data. My research journey entailed going down many roads; more than once,

I needed to turn around. In this process, I encountered several of the previously discussed defense mechanisms (including obstructing and hiding), which slowed my progress.

For instance, I tried to analyze anonymized trends in card "swipes" of all residents (i.e., faculty, student, and staff) across locations to get a more solid grasp of people's physical circulation patterns on campus. First, I was told I could access these data; later, however, my access evaporated. Similarly, I requested anonymized student evaluations of faculty members (i.e., the ratings given by students after each class), particularly sorted by gender and race. Such evaluations were a possible indicator of how students might be contributing to the policing of faculty's behavior. But this request was also deemed off-limits by the dean's office.

Besides such obstructions, hiding defenses sometimes forced me to backtrack. For example, the school preferred to hide, it seems, the circumstances of some faculty members' departures. The oddest rumor I heard was that HBS had historically hired private investigators to conduct background checks on candidates before granting them tenure. An untenured professor had allegedly left after a legal settlement involving that precise issue. I could never confirm this since a nondisclosure agreement supposedly prevented details becoming public. Regardless of the rumor's veracity, this story fed into the school's moral narrative: only vetted and implicitly above-reproach people became part of the inner circle.

Alongside the above defenses, silence was one of the most noticeable modes of faculty socialization. And this mode was particularly clear regarding the very moral issues that I was trying to investigate. This reliance on silence rests on an embrace of moral relativism that is not unique to HBS. This stand, also promoted by many "business ethicists" (including ministers, journalists, professors, and business leaders), entails that "answers to moral questions cannot be correct or mistaken *tout court*, but that they can be correct or mistaken relative to something. In particular, they can be true or false *for* one particular group, society, culture, community, and even person, yet not true for others."[15] For such a view to prevail, silence needs to be the primary engine of any moral pursuit. And in this idealized worldview, only an individual person can and should take a moral position. Carol's reply to the caller about her decision to teach the next day exemplified this viewpoint. It was the caller's silence that allowed her to make the "proper" choice.

Teaching notes used by HBS to socialize faculty illustrate this line of defense well. These notes are typically ten- to fifteen-page documents, available only to school faculty members and other registered instructors, which provide precise guidance on how to conduct a classroom session on a given HBS case. Cases might focus, for example, on a leader's imprint on a company ("GE's Two Decade Transformation: Jack Welch's Leadership") and a given employee's career ("Rob Parsons at Morgan Stanley"). Each of these would be accompanied by unique teaching notes, generally written by the faculty member who developed and first taught the case. Taken together, these HBS cases constitute "heroic folk tale cycles"[16] that students rely on to develop an appreciation of business challenges, and the notes help instructors impart the moral of the tale. Like a map, these notes provide a lens through which to see, read, and navigate the case data, as well as act as an "exemplar" of how teaching should proceed.[17] They literally show junior faculty members what to do when walking into an intimidating ninety-person MBA classroom. Most junior faculty members at the school learn the tricks of their new trade by using these notes, in conjunction with discussions with senior colleagues and preparatory teaching meetings.[18]

While teaching notes offer a model on how to teach, they mostly refrain from specifying what guides individuals' decisions. Indeed, many, though not all, HBS students seem to aspire to engage with something more than the mastery of technical tools. And yet, the notes leave unscripted any broader goals. Teaching notes occasionally allude to such goals (e.g., creating jobs and bolstering a country's competitiveness). But the articulation of broader goals is mostly left to the imagination of faculty members and students. Teaching notes essentially refrain from scripting such aspirations; almost by design, they allow multiple goals to coexist. This relatively hands-off stance leaves participants with the option, if exercised, of filling the gap. The absence of a shared norm should not be understood, however, as the absence of an ideology. To be clear, promoting moral relativism or a what can pass as an non-ideology is also a form of ideology, since it forbids members from forcefully voicing opinions they believe might apply to *all* members of the collective.[19]

This "big tent" approach and desire to accommodate multiple moral viewpoints is apparent throughout the school's history. For example, Charles Gragg, a school faculty member who authored a 1940 teaching note titled "Because Wisdom Can't be Told," explained that "the principal object of professional education is to accelerate a student's ability to act in a mature fashion under conditions of responsibility."[20] What constituted a mature fashion was purposely left unspecified. Gragg added, "each student is free to present and hold to his own views" and fill the gaps left in the teaching notes. This implicit moral relativism is also captured by James Bugental in his article, titled "The Silence of the Sky," which used to be distributed to MBA students in a second-year elective course.[21] In it, Bugental wrote, "We look upon the world with questing eyes that search for meaning, and we are turned back upon our questions with no answers. We seek in vain for the value, the virtue, the cause that is ultimate. . . . And still the sky is silent."[22]

Yet teaching notes were only the tip of the iceberg in this heavily engineered setting. Silence similarly permeated many faculty members' other activities.[23] Several other episodes allowed me to see such a pattern. Each episode might seem like a small fact in itself, but as the sociologist Diane Vaughan notes, such "small facts" can encapsulate larger belief systems.[24]

Early on in my classrooms, I personally made a few missteps before understanding what was expected of HBS faculty members.[25] One case discussion centered on a factory line. I asked my students what the factory's line manager's worst fear might be; one hand quickly went up and, after I called upon the student, he answered, "A union." When pressed to elaborate, he explained that a strike led by a union would stop the lines. The class fell silent and no other hands were raised. At that time, I had not yet learned to wait for other students to pick up on the last comment. I stepped in and reminded the class about the pros and cons of unions across countries and industries; I may have even inserted a comment on the New York City 1911 Triangle Shirtwaist Factory fire and ensuing safety regulations. My views became evident, and the class discussion never really restarted. In the future, I knew not to be as vocal if I wanted students to express themselves in a more HBS-like manner in class.

In addition, in my pursuit of the school's moral compass as a research topic, other school members also initially surrounded me with silence, so as to allow me to make the "right" call of my own volition (i.e., *not* write about the school). The moment I really picked up on such a silence occurred in an internal meeting, during which one of my mentors at the school asked me to discuss my progress on the research project. Paying close attention to silences often proves key to understanding field settings and resistance. In this meeting, three senior faculty members attended, but only two spoke. During close to an hour, with only four of us in a conference room, one poker-faced senior colleague sat there across from me without uttering a word. Such a stand was hard to ignore, but when I asked another participant why this person had shown up to say nothing, silence again met my question. I should know better than to ask, was the implicit message.

This hushed manner of dealing with interlopers echoes, and is probably typical of, the ways many other elite universities handle troubling people or topics: see, for instance, the cultural norms of silence surrounding historical issues of discrimination in admissions against certain demographic groups (such as Jews and Blacks).[26] Nonetheless, given HBS's avowed higher moral aims, the silence on proper conduct proved, over time, distinct and even deafening to my ears. When I failed to make the right call—in this case, presumably stopping my project, or at least "pausing it" till after tenure (as a senior colleague once suggested)—other school members tried to silence me more forcefully.[27]

In 2012, I had finished drafting a book manuscript on HBS faculty socialization and shared it with the dean's office in an effort to be transparent. Nobody had officially asked to vet the manuscript. But some faculty members had expressed fears of a breach of HBS confidential information or other faculty members' privacy when making the results public. As a courtesy, and because I did not view my pursuit as being an underground one, I decided to share the manuscript prior to publication, without promising to incorporate any changes. To my surprise, the dean's office told me than an advisory faculty committee would review the manuscript's contents and inform me of any potential such breaches. The idea of such a committee startled me, since I had already received a green light from the university's Institutional Review Board to conduct the study. Moreover, such a step raised concerns in my mind about academic freedom. I nonetheless agreed to the proposed committee's consultation to the Dean's office and to review a copy of its report so I could decide whether to act upon it. That design seemed to protect my academic freedom.

Again, the idea of "independently" deciding on one's "proper" moral route was the preferred path of action at the school. Colleagues would voice their opinions, and I would then follow the "right" path forward, on my own. Or so the expectation went.

Several weeks later, I received the committee's report. Three readers had combed the pages of the manuscript and produced their assessments. I felt grateful (though a bit embarrassed) that they had spent so much time reading it. A first reader "found no evidence" of breach in data confidentiality or faculty privacy and expressed regrets that I did not discuss the school's ethical curriculum in more depth.[28] A second reader listed a dozen potential items that gave them pause. These ranged from what they described as my overly narrow view of case-writing (e.g., "failure to mention anything about course development as a scholarly pursuit and its relevance to the promotion process") to what was perceived as my flawed view of the school's promotion process (e.g., "the subheading 'Russian Roulette' [that I had used] and the vignette that describes it strike me as overly inflammatory and unnecessarily provocative"). The manuscript "nevertheless . . . largely rings true," admitted this reader, "although it is clearly limited by the 'view from below' [i.e., that of an untenured faculty]." The third reader had no major issues with confidentiality and privacy, besides flagging a few items to look more closely into, including whether students' name cards were visible in photographic illustrations.

More interestingly, this third reader scolded me for not informing my research director that I was working on this project. (The research director is a role held by a senior faculty member to oversee faculty's research progress and budgets at the school.) The reader noted that the project did not appear in my list of ongoing projects or planned output in January 2011 or 2012 and did not come up during those years in my annual discussion with the research director. "I'm disappointed that Michel didn't mention this work," the reader remarked.[29]

This reader's last comment was probably spot on. As early as 2008, I wrote in my report to the dean that I was considering the project and, that same year, engaged in an open departmental discussion of the project with close to thirty colleagues.[30] But by 2011 and 2012, I had experienced so many attempts to silence me that I grew tired of spending so much effort defending it internally. I felt that I had done more than enough to try to convince reluctant insiders. By then, I had also likely gathered that the best way to advance was, thereafter, not to talk too often or too openly about it. The irony of being scolded for behaving exactly as expected (i.e., being silent) did not escape me. In a reversal of blame, the interloper became the culprit rather than the context silencing him.

Silencing's Implications for Interlopers

A key implication of silencing is its ability to isolate interlopers. Indeed, silencing brings *all other* field participants together. Many other defenses require some coordination, but rarely on such a large scale. Silence is like a social glue that binds many people together. The solidarity created by silence is vast and empowering: knowing that others know, yet don't speak up, creates a shared secret with strong implications.

Seeing someone abstain from saying what we know they know creates a joint trajectory, perhaps even a common destiny. Changing course—by breaking the silence—becomes increasingly difficult. In parallel, the need to close ranks and perpetuate the silence seems more and more indispensable. Interlopers themselves can get caught up in these dynamics and rapidly become isolated.

I often wonder how writing about HBS's silence while still being on its faculty might have shaped my findings. Awareness of these dynamics is not, in itself, enough to prevent them from playing out. For instance, I recall going back and forth several times with my editor on the book's title: he felt that the name "Harvard Business School" should be in the title. I felt strongly that it should not, rationalizing that the study needed to go beyond the school and depict more universal patterns. (The name did not appear in the final English title.) In retrospect, perhaps I was merely still trying to belong to the community I was about to leave, and implicitly enforcing its norms by scrubbing away any reference to the school's name from my title to give it less exposure and, implicitly, enforce some kind of silence. Was this an ultimate attempt to belong? It's hard to say, but I cannot discount the possibility. Silence, despite its unsavoriness, still creates a tempting community, which can appeal to those in need of belonging. At that time, I had not yet identified a new community or "holding environment" to join;[31] and this situation might have made me particularly vulnerable to these sirens of belonging.

As hinted above, the silencing of interlopers (such as field researchers) often hinges on the participation of many field members. "Conspiracies of silence," notes sociologist Eviatar Zerubavel, "revolve not around unnoticeable matters we simply overlook but actually around highly conspicuous ones we actively avoid."[32] Actively avoiding a matter necessitates the buy-in of most—if not all—participants in a given field. A mass socialization or indoctrination effort to pressure people to actively disregard a matter must therefore be pursued if silence is to succeed. A telling example noted by Zerubavel is the "infamous US military 'Don't ask, don't tell' policy, designed to prevent those inside it from speaking [about homosexuality] as well as those outside it from hearing."[33] He labels it an "unmistakably collaborative construction built by gays and straights together," both inside and outside the military, so as to stress the scope of participation needed in such conspiracies of silence. He adds that the more numerous those in the know, the better silence is maintained. A first key to success when trying to enforce a code of silence is to ensure that as many participants as possible are "enrolled" in the silent pursuit.

At the same time, it's not the participation of just any kind of person that's sought out. A second key to success when trying to uphold silence is to enroll as many *similar* members as possible in the pursuit. Most examples of well-kept (silent) "open secrets" rest on members' relative uniformity.[34] Indeed, the more uniform the composition of a field's membership, the more easily silence is enforced. Fields that promote silencing need therefore to carefully select their members and protect themselves from the inadvertent entry of future interlopers.

Many analysts of field settings where silence seems to prevail have noted the interplay between members' uniformity and ease of enforcement. As the author Marie Keenan remarks in her study of sexual abuse in the Catholic Church, a distinctive (organizational) feature of the Roman Catholic clergy is that they are "all male, similarly educated, subject to the same authority, professing one belief, and vowing obedience to one supreme head."[35] She also adds that a "total" institution (in the sociologist Erving Goffman's sense) helps sets the tone for silencing.[36] The silencing occurring at HBS to foster proper business conduct (namely, moral relativism) was, without doubt, also enabled by the faculty members' relative uniformity and intense socialization (e.g., via formal parties, dinners, and more). When I was conducting my study, of the 182 tenured and tenure-track faculty members at HBS in 2009, more than 30 percent had received their highest degrees from Harvard University, an incredibly high level of academic inbreeding.[37]

Besides being isolated, those facing a field or an organization trying to silence them risk being incentivized into compliance or exiting the setting. The incentive can take the form of an appointment or even chairing an official committee on the topic of interest. Because a field or an organization then becomes the de facto organizer of—rather than a bystander to—an inquiry, such a move ensures that incumbents retain the power to decide what (if anything) to disclose. There are, however, many other ways to control interlopers: one of them is to literally "pay" them to disappear and implicitly remain silent. When interlopers accept such payments, they then become complicit in the silencing and feel tainted in the process. That feeling is familiar to me.

After my "decision" to opt out of the tenure process and my departure from school, some HBS colleagues there asked me whether I wanted to maintain links with the school (such as being an external reader on doctoral dissertations). My gut reaction has always been "not really," and it still sometimes puzzles me. Here, I suspect that my preference not to reengage suggests more about myself than the school per se. Yet it is also indicative of how silencing, more broadly, operates and how (silenced) interlopers might feel.

Like others at the time, I left the school under quite gener-
ous conditions with a mix of teaching relief and an augmented
research budget. When accepting those conditions, I also felt
that I was tainting myself by agreeing to leave in exchange for
what felt like a too hard-to-resist incentive to withdraw. Thus,
the possibility of renewed links with HBS reminded me of *my*
perceived weakness to have agreed to retreat.

I knew that the way to build my case for staying was to go
up for a full tenure review and then allow any advocates to
build on the likely supportive external letters. At the same
time, I did not want to be a sacrificial lamb going against
the full might of an institution with little interest in keeping
me onboard. Critically, I also did not know how long such
a process might take and whether my record at that time
warranted tenure, since no outside evaluations had been
initiated.

A senior colleague on another Harvard University faculty and
a close observer of HBS dynamics captured well the process of
bribing interlopers into exiting, if not into becoming silent. In a
letter to the University president, they expressed concern about
two specific tenure cases, among others: "Some very strong reap-
pointment and tenure candidates were asked to withdraw prior
to formal departmental review of their files. Each was asked to
withdraw in the spring, shortly after submitting his file and following review by a 3-person, inter-departmental committee.
Outside letters were never solicited. Each was offered a significant inducement to withdraw, contingent on withdrawal . . .
I don't think it should be in the power of anyone to offer an
incentive that is too good to refuse, for this short-circuits the
tenure process."[38]

The feeling of having accepted an incentive—in my view,
also close to a tainted bribe—to exit never really left me. To this
day, being on the HBS campus reminds me of my complicity in

enforcing silence. I suspect other silenced interlopers, in similar situations yet different contexts, share this feeling.

Many scholars know that "just as important as noticing what people say is what they do not say."[39] But there also is a risk of assigning too much importance to what people do not say. When faced with a silencing defense, it is likely easy for field researchers to imbue more meaning than they should into the smallest of perceived "defensive" actions. I hesitate to share the following final story because, logically, I know it cannot be true. Yet the diffuse paranoia that led me to imagine its plausibility might be suggestive of the broader experiences of those being silenced.

In 2014, shortly after the publication of my book on HBS, I received a message from my publisher. Apparently, the *Beijing Times Press* wanted to acquire the simplified Chinese translation rights to my book. I had not heard of this press. While my publisher had never dealt with it either, they reassured me that it was a reputable publishing house. After sending my approval, my publisher sealed the deal within a few days and the foreign press got a window of three years to deliver its translation. During the next few years, I heard nothing. Such a lag may be typical in the publishing world, but for someone who felt previously silenced, it grew suspiciously long.

Becoming more intrigued, I started looking in 2017 at what this foreign press had published. One of the first books I found published by a press with a similar name was what appeared to be a buoyant study of China's current president. In another search, I also found that a similar-sounding press had released transcripts of past Chinese National People's Congress presidiums. The reason such a press would want to acquire translation rights to my book puzzled me. When the translation finally landed on my publisher's desk, just prior to the expiration of the contract, I forwarded it to a Chinese friend. She read it and warned me that the translation was extremely poor, to the point where the text was often unintelligible.

Was this another way to silence me? I remember thinking. Would anyone go to such length as to purchase foreign rights in one of the largest foreign markets for the HBS brand, wait until the expiration of the contractual obligation, and purposely butcher the translation to bury any potential readership? Obviously, this made no sense. But the likelihood (even infinitesimal) of it happening did cross my mind. My contract allowed me to object to its release, so I did that; and I relied on another Chinese friend to help smooth the translation. Ultimately, a revised and improved translation was released a year later.

In retrospect, this translation experience is likely a typical one. Foreign presses scan releases for books that they think might gain broader readership. When they see that the audience remains limited to academics, they refrain from acting until the end of their contract and then rapidly commission a fast translation to retain the rights. But for interlopers facing repeated field defenses, any perceived action taken in such a context can trigger more mixed emotions than justified. I can certainly see how my overreaction to a nonevent was situated in a broader sense of suspicion vis-à-vis imagined field gatekeepers.

Other fieldworkers report similar reactions when reexamining their field interactions. As an illustration, the anthropologist Katherine Verdery discovered after the fact that during her fieldwork in Ceausescu's Romania, many of those she believed to be "friends" reported on her to the secret police because they deemed her a possible spy. After this discovery, Verdery naturally revisited that period in her career. As she explains, such a revisiting yielded "unpleasant and contradictory reactions—bafflement, depression, rage—that I have had to tame."[40] She quickly adds that she has also sought to "tamper anger with gratitude for what they [these friends] were willing to teach me."

With some distance, I realize that revisiting my reaction to the Chinese translation episode is an experience I should perhaps feel more grateful for. It was useful in illuminating the possible inner workings of a defense mechanism reliant on silence and present across fields. While my slight paranoia still feels raw at times, it is now more intelligible and generative.

CHAPTER FIVE

Forgetting

THE TRUTH WAS that I was getting nowhere in my dissertation research. Several days per week, for more than a month, I had been coming to the French aircraft engine manufacturing plant that I was hoping to study. And yet, after all these weeks, I still had not landed any interviews, except for the one with my key contact. The snowball sampling, so elegantly described and praised in the fieldwork manuals that I had read during graduate school, failed to materialize. Days had gone by with the only highlights of my field visits being the train ride from Paris to the nearby commuter rail station, borrowing my mother-in-law's car parked on the station's parking lot, and driving through the morning mist to the plant.

Despite repeated exchanges with Jeannette—my key contact at the plant's labor council and that "first person" supposed to lead me on to the elusive yet "highly desirable" snowball sample—I was hitting a wall.[1] My doctoral defense deadline was looming on the horizon, and my funding was scheduled to expire soon. I was feeling anxious. What if I could never gain access to this plant? Would I need to pack up and find another field site? More importantly, where else would I go? And how long would it take?

That's when Alain, a retired craftsman, walked into the plant's labor council building. It was here where Jeannette, the council's communication manager, had invited me to hang out for the past month. Alain appeared in the main room as I was trying to busy myself, hoping to justify my increasingly useless and awkward presence there. His rugged hands, coupled with his impeccable dress and proud demeanor, signaled to me that it was likely he was a craftsman (as opposed to an unskilled laborer).

Jeannette was ever eager to help me or, by then, perhaps just to get rid of me. So, when she saw the craftsman arrive from her open office door, she warmly teased him about not coming often enough to visit her. He disappeared in her office, and they exchanged news. When they both exited, Jeannette introduced me, like she had done in the past weeks with everyone she thought might want to talk to me. Alain was retired and now a volunteer at the nearby factory museum. (I had visited this museum during one of my early field trips). He offered to show me around his workshop at the museum. Never one to turn down an occasion to connect with plant members, I of course agreed.

Alain was restoring an old engine, one that I knew the firm had developed in the 1970s with a US partner, General Electric (GE). But when I asked him whether he had been to the United States, he brushed my question off as irrelevant. This surprised me a bit, since my father-in-law—who also worked at the plant, and at a lower rank than Alain—had bragged more than once about his travels there and how beautiful Seattle was. Instead, Alain described how the engine had ensured the success of the French (and European) civilian aircraft industry. When I also probed whether US engineers had come to the plant, he told me he could not remember. But again, my father-in-law had told me about Americans coming to work with him and others at the plant. Alain's blind spot created an uneasy interruption in the flow of our conversation. Soon, my other questions, on the engine's compressor, had put us back on track and allowed me to continue conversing with him.

Looking back at my field notes and puzzled reactions to Alain's blind spot, I suspect that's the precise moment I finally started to realize that my *own* American affiliation was much more problematic than I had imagined for this study. I knew that many French people I interacted with, including fellow academics, often held ambivalent views on my US affiliation. The United States was both envied and feared: its large universities' apparent domination, in particular, created both opportunities and challenges for many French academic counterparts. The same held true for its large companies: their achievements were praised and dreaded in French industry.

But that day, with Alain's failure to remember his encounters with US engineers, I sensed that more was at stake. It was as if a sudden amnesia had incapacitated part of Alain's brain. He could recall the exact dates of specific events I inquired about (like the first test-flight of an engine or its key technical modifications over time) and the historical details of a given engine he was refurbishing. Yet apparently, he could not remember anything related to his plant's collaboration with a US company. Alain's unique form of field defense was particularly salient in the peculiar context of this plant (described next). Specifically, Alain's individual amnesia echoed other plant members' preferred way of collectively handling what I would discover to be their fear of dependency on a foreign entity or country.

Yet forgetting is not unique to this setting. What matters most, when faced with such pushback, is understanding what is being forgotten and why. Telling dynamics that shed new light on field participants' unique behaviors often lie beyond the surface of defense mechanisms such as forgetting. The plant's long history largely shaped those dynamics. Even if the plant seemed, from afar, like many others I had seen in France, its distinctive history and dynamics of forgetting were shared by all plant members. The amnesia was collective.

Just outside the gates of the aeronautics plant lay large agricultural fields, mostly barren at that time of year. I remember them well. In the early mornings when I drove past them to see Jeannette, I used to tell myself that at least the mist was beautiful, even if I could not gain actual access to the plant. The mist looked like millions of vaporous strands of cotton hovering above the fields. I often tried to convince myself that this sight itself was enough to make my day. Unfortunately, such wishful thinking did not derail my sense of constantly hitting a wall, at least until my chat with Alain.

Each past visit, as I had walked into the labor council's space outside the plant, the loud and cheerful voice of Jeannette greeted me. She smiled as always when seeing me, and we exchanged small talk. She inquired about what I had tried to do, whom I had reached out to since we last spoke, and invariably offered to put in a good word for me. Alas, her power seemed limited. Here, my key contact's "insider/outsider" role—namely, being a woman in a mostly male manufacturing world—usually highly valued, had not yielded its miracles.[2]

Jeannette's colleagues still eyed me with suspicion. They wondered why a New York University doctoral student was spending so much time snooping around their plant. Had I really come all the way from the United States, inquired several plant members, just to ask them seemingly random questions on their jobs and careers? Could it be that I was more of an undercover agent than a researcher, given that the plant built some plane engines for the French military? If so, it would not be the first time that a fieldworker has been confused for a spy.[3]

It did not help my case that what I was particularly interested in was clandestine: specifically, my research focused on retirement gifts, illegally made by members for personal use on company time and with company materials. Miniature rockets, small elaborate engines, and other intricate metal artifacts capturing the lives of retiring craftsmen—I was told—lined the shelves of almost all highly trained retirees in technical areas. Jeannette could easily recall the many retirement parties she had attended over the years where these sometimes beautiful creations were unveiled. She even showed me photos of some of these pieces. But the only ones I had ever seen were those in the home of my father-in-law, which he had received on other occasions (e.g., an end-of-project celebration).

Yet despite my best efforts, and before my episode with Alain, I had failed to speak to anyone, besides my father-in-law, who had actually built or received such a gift. The closest I came to seeing one that my relative did not own was in an antique shop near the plant. It was a wonderfully crafted, brushed steel ceiling lamp. The shop owner was evasive about how he had acquired it or who had left it with him. He only seemed intent on selling it to me, its origin unspoken. That initially promising lead led nowhere.

When spending time with Jeannette—whether in her office, or in a nearby large open space where plant members dropped in during their breaks, or at lunch for various council activities—she would invariably introduce me to anyone roaming in the vicinity. She told people that I wanted to connect with them to understand the folklore surrounding these artifacts. In short, "He's conducting an oral history of the plant," was her main pitch to get me in the door. People coming through the council to order tickets for social outings, inquire about summer camps for their kids, or borrow books (all activities supported by the council) were briefed on my presence. Consistently, they would listen to her and ask me where I was from and what I was doing. I would answer that I had grown up in France but now lived in New York and was conducting a thesis in an American university on the labor history at the plant.[4] Hoping to ingratiate myself with them, I sometimes insinuated that a family member worked here but never named him, to protect his privacy. They all congratulated me for being interested in their plant. And none of them ever followed up.

This changed after speaking to Alain. The exchange was probably the beginning of my realization that, to better fit into this field, perhaps I had to mimic his behavior and scrub my affiliation with the United States. It took me some time to master how to do so. Because I had also landed an affiliation with a French university when moving to France to conduct my fieldwork, I often presented myself at the plant as a doctoral student from New York currently affiliated with Sciences Po in Paris.[5] Gradually, I learned that the better way forward was simply to present myself as a researcher with the French university and to omit my US roots.

In retrospect, it's hard to know if that omission allowed me to finally get people to talk to me. What I did notice is that once I became more "French" and less "American," the ease with which I secured interviews dramatically changed. Subsequently, whenever Jeannette introduced me to someone new, I quickly interrupted her to say that I was a researcher at a French university and to prevent her, at least up-front, from talking about my New York ties.

Little did I know that in these early attempts at forgetting my past, I had touched upon one of the key tensions that existed at the plant. Namely, I had stumbled upon the firm's uneasy reliance on, and repeated attempts to forget, the foreign experts—engineers from the United States, Austria, and Germany—that had proven central to building a "French" aeronautics industry.[6]

After I toured Alain's workshop and continued learning about his work in the plant prior to retiring, he slowly introduced me to his friends—mostly other retirees who would come to see him there. He always told them I was a student at Sciences Po. All traces of my US lineage had conveniently vanished. Granted, the Sciences Po affiliation carries prestige in France, but so does an affiliation with a foreign university, like New York University. This new way of depicting me perhaps rendered me more "native" to their eyes.

I didn't fully realize it at the time, but this makeover of sorts taught me what Alain and his coworkers knew all too well: in this instance, forgetting foreign associations proved best. Otherwise, memories of decades of foreign involvements at the plant were likely to bubble up, which apparently no one was keen to remember. The only way of taming them was to remember to forget them, in the same way that Alain had forgotten my non-French past. This form of field resistance to part of an interloper's perceived identity proved critical to my inquiry.

SNECMA's Fear of Being Perceived as Unpatriotic

The plant's history helps illuminate how my presence might have triggered Alain's odd behavior. Ever since the end of World War II, the military conquest of the skies has held a special place in France's national imagination. Indeed, industry observers saw Germany's ability to design and manufacture powerful engines for its military airplanes as contributing to France's initial defeat during the war.[7] To ensure that history would not repeat itself, right after the end of the war in 1945, the French government created by executive order the firm SNECMA (Société Nationale d'Études et de Construction de Moteurs d'Aviation). The company—which would go on to employ my father-in-law, Jeannette, Alain, and hundreds of others—represented France's main answer to developing a national aeronautics capability, particularly in the face of growing competition from foreign engine manufacturers (such as GE, Pratt & Whitney, and Rolls-Royce).

Of course, the company sought out operational success. But beyond that, nothing was more important to SNECMA's management than to become an independent world industry leader in engine manufacturing, so as to answer France's call.[8] There was only a small problem with this patriotic aspiration. For multiple decades after its creation, SNECMA actively sought out and collaborated extensively with foreigners to survive in this competitive market.[9]

More specifically, two foreign involvements proved key to the firm's survival. First, from 1945 to 1970, SNECMA heavily recruited and relied on German engineers to help France catch up with other nations in producing military engines. Many of these individuals had worked for the German military (supposedly with better aeronautics expertise than the French one) and could therefore teach SNECMA how to improve its engines. Second, from 1970 to 2000, SNECMA joined forces with the US-based GE to build a family of civilian engines, which resulted in steady civilian sales. SNECMA even signed a licensing agreement with GE, allowing it to manufacture these engines in France. Despite being presented as a fully joint collaboration of equal partners, some saw the agreement as validating SNECMA's subordinate (subcontracting) role vis-à-vis GE.

All these foreign involvements were key to SNECMA's growing market share. Still, they also challenged the idea that SNECMA was a truly French company. When individuals (such as government officials and labor union representatives) raised questions on the company's patriotic achievement, SNECMA was quick to defend its record—a response facilitated by the systematic omission of any element perceived as contradictory to the firm's official history. For more than five decades, the firm repeatedly forgot to mention in its official communications the key role foreigners had played in helping SNECMA secure its industry position.

Such forgetting might seem quite anecdotal if it did not teach us a lot about what company leaders feared the most: namely, to be seen as losing in technological and industrial prowess to foreign competitors, especially those that might eventually prove enemies of the country. Scrubbing the company's history of the critical German and US involvement allowed SNECMA to appear more independent and therefore uphold the belief that it helped France retain its "grandeur" (or what the historian Gabrielle Hecht, in her study of the French nuclear industry, calls the country's industrial "radiance").[10]

A deeper dive into the company's history is necessary to fully grasp why SNECMA's leaders were so concerned about being seen as unpatriotic. Many key decision-makers in government and influential labor union leaders were quick to point out possible unpatriotic behaviors. And so, forgetting was a protective way for SNECMA to barricade itself gradually, but solidly, against such claims. By ensuring that its historical record was clean of foreign taint, plant members could more easily dismiss any challenges both from within and outside. As a mechanism of defense, SNECMA's forgetting is probably exemplary. Yet many other workplaces engage in similar defenses on a probably smaller and less systematic scale. But in SNECMA's case, the consistency and longevity of the efforts to forget still astound me.

An Embarrassing Reliance on Foreign Expertise

At its core, SNECMA was supposed to represent a new image of France: one that would erase France's humiliating military defeat at the start of World War II and the shameful collaboration between the French government of Vichy and the German occupying forces. All these dynamics saddled SNECMA with a heavy burden, even at its inception, as a firm that in itself needed to prove its patriotism. Even more problematically, the main preexisting manufacturer that formed the core of the new SNECMA violated that required patriotism: in fact, the French provisional government had labeled it as "unpatriotic" because of its close work with Germans during the war.[11] Rather than heroically resisting the occupying force, SNECMA's main absorbed entity had instead embraced it. So not only did SNECMA need to live up to its creators' high hopes, but it had to do so while inheriting, at birth, an embarrassing past.

The large French flag at full mast blowing in the wind in front of the plant was not enough to alleviate the fear of being seen as unpatriotic. The unease about not appearing "French" enough permeated the firm's subsequent history and behavior. Almost a decade after its inception, SNECMA still needed to assert its importance, promising readers of its annual report that the company possessed "a fully autonomous and path-breaking technology allowing it to be counted among the leading engine manufacturers in the world."[12] Even with the US collaboration going full steam in the mid-1980s, a company representative felt the need to assert publicly that the firm had fulfilled the mission assigned to it in 1945, namely, to "reposition France in the arena of aeronautics engines."[13] These pronouncements and other evidence suggest a keen awareness by SNECMA members of the firm's mandate and, at the same time, of the felt necessity to preemptively defend themselves against any unpatriotic insinuations.

What complicated SNECMA's already perilous early trajectory was how the French government jump-started SNECMA's development and manufacture of military engines in 1945: by deciding to hire 120 engineers from Germany and Austria.[14] It was these engineers—also known as the "O group" in reference to their leader's last name (Oestrich)—that almost single-handedly positioned SNECMA as a crucial supplier to the French Air Force.[15] And they did so by developing and producing SNECMA's ATAR engine, which could be directly traced to the engine these same engineers had worked on while still in Berlin and helping the German military.

Everyone at SNECMA, of course, celebrated the engine's launch in 1948. But its roots and origins were never spotlighted. It is true that France and SNECMA were not alone: several other countries, including the United States and the USSR, also enrolled German engineers into their national industrial pursuits after World War II, with no questions asked about their links to the Nazis.[16] SNECMA was therefore not an outlier. Even so, the tension around this history persisted at SNECMA and triggered a unique response: systematic forgetting.

The structural omission from the company's official history of these engineers' presence, not to mention their role in SNECMA's success, is most obvious in internal company bulletins. An analysis of more than three hundred of these bulletins (i.e., internal newsletters for employees) published between 1953 and 1999 shows that out of the 5,622 pages printed, only five pages mention or allude to the German and Austrian presence at SNECMA.[17] For instance, upon the leader Oestrich's retirement in 1960, the bulletin most explicitly refers to this past by reproducing an internal memorandum signed by SNECMA's director praising Oestrich's contributions to "the difficult Franco-German collaboration" (with no further explanations). Apart from this and other limited references, the foreign involvement left little trace in the bulletins. Such omissions were puzzling given that the bulletins covered all SNECMA-related topics, ranging from company events like minor social gatherings to new engine developments. A former SNECMA union representative also noted what he called SNECMA's leaders' "more or less conscious desire to 'erase' the German presence" from the firm's memory.[18] Many other public portrayals of the company (e.g., annual reports) similarly omit this past.

Considering these omissions, it was almost by chance that I stumbled upon the extent of the German collaboration at the plant. Working off a list of plant retirees given to me by Jeannette, I sent letters to their home addresses explaining my study around retirement gifts and asking for an interview. The most moving reply came from a widow whose retired husband had just passed away. She noted in a letter she sent me how much the job had meant for him and how proud he had been of his work. She also included a picture of the retirement gift he received. It looked truly unique. I initially thought of simply thanking her for her reply and moving on, since she did not fit my "sample" (i.e., active or retired craftsmen). Fortunately, I reconsidered and met her one afternoon in her home. Beautifully carved wooden miniature planes adorned her shelves. Rarely had I seen so many and such elegant examples of illegally

produced artifacts at the plant, also ones that were not presented only as departure gifts.[19]

When she recounted her husband's career and their life
together, she mentioned the name of a small town in the center
of France where they had lived. By chance, years back, a work
assignment brought me to that town for several weeks. We discussed the town's unique layout as a former island on the Loire
River and the beauty of its surroundings. Upon sharing the
name of the hotel I had stayed in with her, she paused. "That's
where the German engineers [hired by SNECMA after World
War II] initially stayed," she softly replied, "before finding
more permanent housing." She then told me about how her
husband had trained under their supervision. Her indirect
affiliation to the plant combined with the mourning of her
husband's passing might have liberated her speech. That conversation was the first time I heard anything about Germans
working at the plant. Till then, all craftsmen I had spoken to
had omitted this possibly objectionable past.

This was not, however, the only episode that craftsmen
omitted from their past. Once SNECMA and its members had
almost managed to distance themselves from their "tainted"
German past, another foreign involvement (the new collaboration with GE in the 1970s) reignited the same unease. With
a playbook on how to deal with an embarrassing past now
implicitly established, SNECMA's employees replicated what
they had learned earlier and started forgetting the US collaboration as well. (This forgetting was exactly how Alain had
brushed off my question on travels to the US and claimed not
to remember the presence in France of any GE engineers.)

Looking again at the internal bulletins produced for employees and other readers, a similar pattern of omissions surfaces.
Out of the almost three hundred pages related to GE-related
activities, only a small number (eighteen pages, or 0.3 percent)

dealt specifically with the GE collaboration—despite it representing a significant part of SNECMA's business. In a rare public acknowledgment of the firm's dependence on GE, SNECMA estimated that 34 percent of its revenues in 2004 flowed from GE-related collaborations.[20] But overall, SNECMA was extremely adept at forgetting this past and quick to ensure, at least till the early 2000s, that no mention was made of the collaboration.

SNECMA's handling of its patriotic mandate in light of foreign involvements exemplifies what can be learned from analyzing such forgetting. Such an examination of this mode of field resistance proves indicative of the unique challenges that participants face. And many other fields deploy similar efforts to forget issues that they deem challenging to deal with. Consider the case of US universities that trace their wealth to slavery. Current university leaders and members often hold their initial founders and benefactors in great esteem. Still, these universities' official records generally omit these same individuals' more embarrassing involvement with enslavement.[21]

Outside of academia, other settings exhibit similar forgetting dynamics. For instance, companies absorbed by others of a lesser status but in the same industry (e.g., an investment bank acquired by a commercial bank but retaining its historical name) might prove quick to forget their new ownership, since it could threaten their former credentials. Forgetting is a versatile and telling tool used to cover many forms of contestation.

Forgetting's Implications for Interlopers

Like silencing, forgetting generally requires a constant policing of the many that are directly and indirectly in the know of an issue. When an issue is as widespread as the one alluded to above (i.e., an infusion of more than a hundred engineers in a midsize company), the sheer number of people in the know can grow exponentially. Not only those directly involved but also those living or working with them are aware of the contentious dynamics.

In the case of SNECMA's hiring of German and Austrian engineers, their families were also resettled in France.[22] Moreover, many spouses of the Frenchmen working alongside the Germans (including the widow I interviewed) knew about their husbands' work. At minimum, several hundred people were therefore directly and indirectly in the know. Despite the French government's best efforts to resettle everyone in a remote location (the town in which I had spent time) and keep the foreigners mainly together as work teams, their presence hardly went unnoticed.[23]

The policing of SNECMA's past needed to occur constantly: inside and outside of the workplace, in formal and informal settings, and over careers that might extend for decades. Any slippage could allow the fear of unpatriotic behavior to suddenly resurface. Constantly remembering to forget was the default behavior among current and past plant members as well as among most of their relatives.

For example: in the early 1980s, there was a retirement ceremony of a French engineer who had worked closely with the Germans at SNECMA. The retiree's supervisor gave a speech underlining the fact that the retiree had entered the aeronautics industry as a "mere draftsman." But that was not true. In fact, the retiree *had* previously graduated from an aeronautics engineering school, but that school was in Germany, and he attended it during World War II. His supervisor knew this yet preferred to omit this key, German element of his past to avoid any slippage.[24]

Under such circumstances, efforts to forget are contained with difficulty to a specific moment or segment of field participants. Like a royal court where everyone is groomed into behaving properly, all field participants or members in an organization need to be taught how to behave with respect to the contentious issue.[25] In particular, each new wave of entrants or recruits need to learn from interacting with their more senior peers that some past events should never be discussed openly. The socialization never really stops, though it does offer multiple occasions for slippage.

A first implication of forgetting is that all field participants— including interlopers—need to be continuously on their guard when interacting with others around the contentious topic. For example, I wondered once whether going to the plant by driving a car *not* built by a French automaker might mark me as suspicious. I had noticed that most cars on the outside parking lot were either Renault, Peugeot, or Citroën brands. Without fully articulating the connection, I recall associating this predominance of French brands with the factory's past and its insistence on its patriotic mission. Even such seemingly tangential details suddenly took on a new contrast once I discovered what needed to be forgotten.

The parking lot was often busier than I expected. Craftsmen meticulously maintained their vehicles and could often be seen hanging around a shiny new (French-built) car that one of them brought in, chatting about its details, and even peering inside its open hood. Alain's car, for instance, looked as if it had come directly out of a car wash each time I saw him there. The equivalent of the office water-cooler chats here occurred mostly around parked cars.[26]

My mother-in-law's car—which I borrowed each time I drove to the plant—initially proved ideal. It was a French-built Peugeot 205 and blended in perfectly with the other cars on the plant's parking lot. (She worked in Paris and had an opposite commute, allowing me to use the car she left at the train station during the day.) I felt I could proudly drive my mother-in-law's car in plain view without any need to forget it. Clearly, it was not beautiful, but it fit the patriotic bill, and it even counterbalanced my suspicious affiliation with the United States. But on one occasion I could not borrow my usual car and needed to find an alternative. A friend's Japanese-built model was my only option. That day, I consciously made sure to park as far as possible from the labor council's main doors and tried to hide the vehicle behind a much larger one.[27]

Forgetting might seem easy. But, in fact, it requires constant remembering—even on the part of interlopers like myself—if they want to "properly" remain in a field and pursue their inquiry. They need to remain actively aware of what to cognitively cordon off. Constantly scanning the field for clues that trigger the learned behavior becomes second nature. Even when engaging in apparently mundane acts, the fear of committing blunders looms relentlessly.[28]

A second implication for interlopers dealing with fields and organizations prone to forgetting is that their efforts might require more archival research than when dealing with other defenses. When properly socialized, core field members might be able to easily forget. Still, for them to *not* produce any historical traces (or even to destroy them) is harder to achieve. After learning from my interview with the widow about the presence of German engineers, I read more carefully any archive concerning this period. In particular, I noticed Oestrich's name repeatedly cited on technical patents associated with engine developments at the firm. Patents could not easily be scrubbed to erase that foreign-sounding name.

Matching patents and engine development timelines, I could see spikes in "development" right after World War II, which led me to look into historians' accounts of SNECMA's early consolidation. It was only after establishing the historical record that I could directly ask my father-in-law about what had previously escaped me: the plant's German DNA. Even he was reluctant to say much beyond simply confirming the past role of the "O" group.[29] That said, the archival traces were much more telling; they allowed me to fill in the missing pieces of the puzzle and write about the plant's tainted past.

Almost a decade after "accessing" this field, I published an article about SNECMA's "unpatriotic" history.[30] It came out in English and seven years after I had left the field. In the same way that the sociologist Loïc Wacquant wrote *Body and Soul* in French—to "achieve increased emotional distance from and analytical clarity about the materials" collected in English on the boxing world—I chose to write in a language other than the one used in my field.[31] This linguistic choice, along with a time lag, likely facilitated my distancing and sharpened my analytical eye when dealing with such "embarrassing" materials. I was writing about a past that some preferred to forget, but in a language and for an audience distant enough from the field to help me not feel too traitorous.

Despite this double distancing (linguistic and temporal), I still feel slightly ambivalent about this reveal. As all fieldworkers well know, "At its core, fieldwork must be regarded as something of a traitorous activity."[32] So it was a relief that few plant members could read my English prose and that I did not revisit the plant (after the article's publication) for my "treason" to be called out. The anthropologist Nancy Scheper-Hughes's recounting of her "traumatic" return to her field site after disclosing what some preferred to keep quiet lingers in my mind. What she describes as "the difficulties of balancing one's responsibility to honest ethnography with care and respect for people who shared a part of their lives and their secrets" are inherent to many field inquiries.[33] Yet the higher the field defenses, the more probable that the reveal will feel tempting, and the more complicated this balancing act is to maintain.

As interlopers try to gain access to fields (and later exit them), unearth forgotten facts, and reveal them to their readers, they might be viewed by other field participants as traitors. But they ultimately are also traitors to *themselves,* since properly socialized interlopers will need to do violence to themselves in order not to forget what should never be publicly revealed. Forgetting helps "build" a community, one the interloper also becomes part of. All those in the know are usually aware of who else knows and therefore develop a sense of shared trajectory.

Defenses are often layered, and I would be remiss not to mention the other defenses that coexisted at this SNECMA plant. For instance, more than once, the firm's management obstructed my access to the plant and suggested that I meet people outside the plant gates instead. Also, several plant members enforced silencing around the topic of foreign involvements. Speaking about anything but French efforts directed towards building plane engines was taboo. That said, forgetting was the most salient defense I encountered in the plant. The rewriting of history proved central to the collective effort to derail any inquiry into a troubling past. No one, however, denied these foreign involvements.

Forgetting together develops a group's cohesion. Many forms of forgetting—including "prescriptive" ones (i.e., in the interest of all parties involved) and ones "constitutive of a new identity" (i.e., a process in which new shared memories are constructed)—create a kinship that projects group members forward rather than letting them dwell on their past.[34] National identities, for example, are prime examples of the generative and future-oriented power of forgetting, since these identities often "combine remembering and forgetting, with a greater emphasis on the latter" as a way to sustain a desired national unity.[35]

In short, forgetting might initially seem merely defensive. But it is also constructive, usefully binding members (including interlopers) together in a way that only a few other forms of defense (such as silencing) permit. The sea of French cars parked on the plant lot perhaps best captures the generative nature of forgetting: every driver's seemingly individual car-purchasing decision aligned to create this vast patriotic tapestry—one that, almost unconsciously, omitted any hint of foreignness. The next and last empirical chapter will conclude this inquiry into field defense mechanisms by showcasing instances of field denials and illuminating their meanings.

CHAPTER SIX

Denying

AS WE PARKED our car on the driveway to the large country house that belonged to an acquaintance who was a writer, I playfully told my spouse—an author himself—writing must pay better than I imagine. The house, where we spent a night on our way back to Paris after a vacation further south, was in a lush and agricultural region of France. From the house's patio, landscaped gardens slowly descended towards a pond and woods. This acquaintance spent most of his summers there and had invited us to drop by. My spouse knew him because they both shared a publisher and had crossed paths at book fairs. I did not know what to expect prior to our arrival. But I certainly had not imagined such a majestic estate. Without missing a beat, my spouse corrected my first impression: the host's late father was a successful architect who had years ago purchased the estate and donated it to his children. Writing does not pay, was the implicit takeaway, at least for now.

That evening, our host's neighbors joined us for dinner. They lived nearby, in a similarly grand country house. The food was delicious, and the conversation enjoyable. Over dinner, I learned more about the neighbors: he was also a writer, she an editor, and together they lived most of the year in Geneva, Switzerland. The combination of their country home and city dwelling, explained the writer, proved ideal for allowing him to write and connect with his publisher when in Geneva. What a wonderful life, I volunteered. His wife concurred: they were lucky to be able to afford such a lifestyle, she added, partially thanks to his writing income. Some writing, it seemed, did in fact pay . . .

Gradually, I came to understand how this improbable financial situation was possible. The neighbor had initially been a bit sheepish about what he did for a living, but our host encouraged him to open up. "We are among writers, right? Don't be afraid," he told him as we settled in the living room after dinner. As trust grew and wine continued to flow, the neighbor explained that he wrote for other people.

"You mean you are a ghostwriter?" I asked. "No," he shot back, "I help others write their books." Increasingly intrigued, I probed, "How many others?" His answer was "mainly one," but it was an author he had "worked with" for over a decade and for several books. (Note his use of the term "with," rather than worked "for.") The conversation moved on to how he did his work and never returned to how he labeled himself. The French word for ghostwriter, however, was *not* one he seemed to appreciate or use.[1] Critically, he denied being one.

At first, I brushed off his denial: our connection was only newly formed, after all, and our exchange had been a bit guarded. What I gathered was that ghostwriting could fuel the lifestyle he and his wife enjoyed. Despite never being acknowledged publicly, he explained that he shared royalties with his author on the books "they" published together. It took a few more glasses of wine for him to disclose the author he "helped." I was stunned by the disclosure. The person was a prominent French author, regularly invited on television and radio shows, with more than forty books to his name. To say that he was a household name would be an understatement. His constant presence on the media scene suddenly could be better explained: if he didn't need to spend much time writing, he could dedicate himself entirely to the books' promotion.

Not only did the neighbor write the initial draft of all the books this author had published in the past decade or so, but he also suggested new book projects. He explained how he came up with proposals, did initial research, and presented various options to his author to see what made the most sense. Together, they went over the possibilities, tried to plan a "production" schedule, and discussed which topics might prove timelier than others to maximize sales. The neighbor did say that he felt a bit left out during the book launches. (Rarely did he ever attend any of these events.) Regardless, the publishers knew him well, since he was named in his author's publishing contract, and they paid him directly, handsomely too it seemed.

Outside the above small circle, the ghostwriter's name rarely circulated. "Who cares," he remarked, "I live the life I want and can work on the projects I wish, writing books that are widely read." "What's not to like?" he added with an upbeat tone, but also a somewhat pensive gaze. Perhaps, I recall thinking, but then what's the necessity to deny being a ghostwriter?

Triggered in part by this encounter, I started years later a collaborative research project on ghostwriters.[2] This neighbor's denial of being a ghostwriter proved more typical than my coauthor and I expected. And it suggested that, despite being mostly invisible to the public, even those who functioned as actual ghostwriters viewed themselves as anything but.

This neighborly encounter was my first informal meeting with a ghostwriter. It immediately taught me not only about such denials but also how *not* to speak about their line of work.

Understanding why this mattered so much to them proved more complicated to grasp, yet ultimately worthwhile, since it shed new light on their entire profession.

Seasoned ghostwriters, in fact, saw themselves almost as artists that create personas, which are identical neither to those of the people they are meant to impersonate nor to their own. What that meant was that ghostwriters viewed themselves as artistic creators of selves. Denials allowed them to affirm those views and correct any misperceptions others might have about their stigmatized job.[3]

To examine ghostwriters' work, the obvious first hurdle, and it was a high one, was finding them. Indeed, most "authors"—also labeled "talents" in the publishing industry's vernacular—tend not to disclose the names of the ghostwriters with whom they work. As such, finding true "ghostwriters" would prove difficult, so we initially focused on those writers that were publicly listed as coauthors of memoirs. Writers listed on the cover of books by celebrities or other prominent talents, explained a few publishing industry insiders, also often ghostwrote entire books without having their names on the cover.

Why were the same writers sometimes on the cover and sometimes not? This was explained by an insider: it depends on how much a talent is willing to fork out. The higher the pay, the more invisible ghostwriters become. Looking for visible gigs could uncover the less visible work of these same writers. We therefore started with the *New York Times* bestseller lists, particularly memoirs, and homed in on memoirs' coauthors (who were not the talents); that's how I met Jeff.[4]

Jeff was the first potential ghostwriter who agreed to formally meet me face-to-face. He lived in Brooklyn, New York, and his coauthored book about a musical celebrity had sold very well. Our email exchanges about it were brief but bubbly.

He seemed open to speaking about his writing experiences, though on his own terms. The impression I got from these exchanges was that I was being hustled a bit. It did not bother me since I was on the lookout for a hard-to-find sample. "Are afternoons OK? Could I select the place to meet?" he inquired. My desire to literally see a potential ghostwriter led me to agree to all his terms.

Jeff and I met in an empty and trendy restaurant near his home on a sunny afternoon. Despite the later hour, he had not yet eaten. Could he order lunch, he asked? "Of course, my treat," I volunteered, in retrospect, a bit too rapidly. As a hired pen used to opting for the highest bidder, he immediately jumped on the occasion and ordered oysters with a glass of wine—not exactly the "coffee" fare I planned on covering out of my pocket. I wondered if he was testing me and trying to see whether my pockets were deep enough for us to talk. Alternatively, he might simply have been trying to signal his worth to me. After some small talk, he dug into his food while I tried to plough through our interview.

We first talked at length about his coauthored books. An hour later, over desert and another glass of wine (his, not mine), I broached the topic of ghostwriting: "What if someone asked you not to list your name on the book? Would that be an option?" Till then, he had only spoken about "cowriting" memoirs and not about ghostwriting. "I'm always up for that, it really does not matter," he added elusively. Pushed to say whether he had done it before, he said he had not, but clarified he would if "it made sense."

By making sense he meant, if "it's someone who's actually done work like that . . . You know, let's say, you know, 70 percent or even 50 percent [of the writing] . . . Even [if] 50 percent was actual written stuff that I could edit that they did, I would feel a bit unjust taking credit and I would be completely fine with a ghostwriting credit. You know, like a thank-you. You can always find out who the ghostwriter is. Usually, they're thanked in the acknowledgments." He seemed very well informed for someone who claimed *not* to be a ghostwriter. I wondered if 50 percent was truly his lower threshold for agreeing to omit his name from the cover.

Trying to get a bit more information before ending our chat, I told him I guessed that perhaps half of the solo-authored memoirs we had identified on the *NYT* bestseller lists might be ghostwritten. Even this number, according to many publishing insiders we had spoken to, was a conservative estimate. He jumped in to correct my estimate: "I mean unless we're talking about somebody like Tina Fey, who's a writer. You know, before she was really on camera, she was writing too. Unless we're talking about somebody like that, I'm going to say they all are [ghostwritten]. At least to some degree. You know? I mean an editor can do it too, but a good editor can jump in and do it. I've seen that happen too." Jeff continued, "There was a book that I kind of wanted to do, and an editor I know, she was doing basically what the work of a ghostwriter would do. And editing it too. I have to be honest, I think it suffered . . . I think a book should have an editor and a writer. And that way you need two sets of eyes. You really do." He seemed to speak from experience.

Whether the writer was visible or not to the public appeared somewhat beside the point, according to him at least. Denials of any kind involve more than one person and are best understood as co-denials that suppose a "mutual avoidance."[5] In the case of Jeff's denial, my presence at lunch offered him an opportunity to deny that he was a ghostwriter and insist on only being a "cowriter."

Statements of denial come in many flavors. In essence, they are "assertions that something did not happen, does not

exist, is not true or is not known about."[6] When field participants repeatedly deny something that seems irrefutable (at
least to outsiders), interlopers need to pay careful attention.
The reasons for such denials require probing. More importantly,
such denials can often open entirely new ways of understanding
a given field. Here, Jeff was not only rejecting my attempt at
labeling him. He was also, crucially, helping me see the more
desirable way for people in his line of work to be recognized
and acknowledged: namely as cowriters and as creators of
other people's selves.

Ghostwriters' Varying and Limited Recognition for Their Work

There are many ways that cowriters can be publicly recognized
for their work. First, at the most visible end of the spectrum, a
cowriter's name can appear on the book's cover, in the same
size and font as the talent's. Such a full "coauthorship" form of
acknowledgment and recognition is rare. One example is
Amanda Lindhout's memoir of her abduction and captivity in
Somalia, cowritten with Sara Corbett.[7]

Second and more often, a cowriter's name appearing on a
cover is listed after the subject's name, preceded by "and" or
"with," so as to suggest a hierarchy in the cowriters. Donald
Trump's memoir exemplifies such a form of shared, yet tiered,
recognition. The cover of *Trump: The Art of the Deal* lists the
book's authors as "Donald J. Trump with Tony Schwartz."[8]

Third, and perhaps more frequently, a cowriter's name can
appear in the acknowledgments section of a book.[9] Andre
Agassi's memoir illustrates such a configuration. At the start of
his acknowledgments, Agassi notes, "this book would not exist
without my friend J. R. Moehringer," adding that he helped
"me tackle my own memoir and give it shape."[10]

Contrasting with all these configurations, and at the least visible end of the spectrum, a cowriter's name can be entirely omitted from the published work. Such a cowriter becomes a ghostwriter in the true sense of the term, in that his or her name is fully shielded from public view. The French ghostwriter whom I had met over dinner fit this profile: his work was invisible to all but a few people.

Given the dynamics of my late afternoon lunch with Jeff, I learned not to begin by asking cowriters whether they were ghostwriters. When approaching potential ghostwriters, I always spoke at length about their other cowriting experiences, before letting the exchange veer towards their less visible work (if any). Oftentimes, such an approach proved quite effective. Here's an example of an exchange with another successful cowriter. Alisha told me that her "contracts are always collaboration agreements between me and the author. The author has a publishing agreement with the house, and I have an agreement with the author. For [Book 3], I received 40 percent of the advance of $125,000. My agent always negotiates everything. In terms of recognition, it varies from project to project. On [Book 3], it was always a 'with [Alisha].'"

The advance is the flat fee paid out to authors (often broken into multiple segments), which is technically an advance against the future anticipated royalties from sales of the book. Importantly, such an advance is paid out regardless of whether the book ever sells enough copies to cover that amount of money. This means the advance is fundamentally a bet. In this case, then, Alisha is functionally paid a flat fee, which is good (since she does not take on risk if the book does not sell) and also bad (should the book she cowrote sell well, she will not see any additional money).

Alisha then continued, "I have fully cowritten five books, and book-doctored two. These were books that had been submitted to the editor but just didn't work. I received cover credit on three out of the five books, and of course nothing for the book-doctoring." (Nothing but a hefty fee!) Book-doctoring is another way to help bring a book to print. Unlike for fully ghost-written books, the book "doctor" usually only stepped in when a book manuscript was already partly or fully drafted. Under such circumstances, the person was treated more as a fixer than a midwife. More importantly, Alisha confirmed that she could be more or less visible depending on the gig and pay.

To better understand why denials are so integral to the work of ghostwriters, an overview of the industry proves key. Ghost-writing is nothing new. As one of the few early "out" ghostwrit-ers, Jane Erdal suggests in her memoir that ghostwriting "might almost qualify as the oldest profession if prostitution had not laid prior claim."[11] (The association with another often-stigmatized line of work already provides some context for Jeff's denial.) What is new, however, is the contemporary growth in demand for ghostwriting services. From shorter pieces (such as articles, blog posts, and other "content marketing" work for businesses and public relations agencies) to longer pieces (such as novels, celebrity cookbooks, personal memoirs, and even academic articles and undergraduate theses), the demand for ghostwriters seems to be on the rise.[12] Perhaps because of this rise, a few other experienced ghostwriters also recently came out and penned "how to" books for aspiring entrants into their profession.[13]

Generally speaking, cowriters (including ghostwriters) sell a product to individuals for whom "written communication isn't their forte" or who "don't have time" to write.[14] As contrac-tors, ghostwriters sign—like Alisha did—a collaboration agree-ment with their subjects, even though editors and publishers can make introductions.[15] This agreement outlines all matters of confidentiality, responsibilities and due dates, copyright, and recognition. It also spells out the agreed compensation: namely, whether cowriters are paid a flat fee or royalties derived from the finished product. Under the former arrangement, cowriters do not hold a copyright on the finished product. Under the latter arrangement, cowriters receive a negotiated share of the product's profits, which can be as much as 50 percent of the author's earnings.

In some instances, the confidentiality agreements were so stringent that cowriters could not even comment on or reply to our requests to be part of our study. In one exchange, for instance, the agent of a very successful ghostwriter I had contacted explained: "Unfortunately, [ghostwriter's name] is unable to participate in this study. She has confidentiality clauses which she must honor. These restrictions include, for the most part, doing interviews which involve any of her clients. We certainly hope you understand." Such clauses created challenges for our research project, but, more importantly, they were also problematic for most of the cowriters we spoke to. Except for the very sought after ones (like the above person who declined to participate), most cowriters need to constantly hustle for their next gig. They are hired hands always on the lookout for who will pay them next, and their working conditions tend to be precarious.[16]

One way for cowriters to find work is through previous connections to publishers and editors. The famous French author's ghostwriter is a good example of this chain of connections. Recall that the neighbor's wife worked in the publishing industry as an editor. Importantly, she had edited one of the ghostwriter's main author's early (presumably, still solo written) books. I later learned that she had been the matchmaker between her husband and this now-famous author. (She had therefore somewhat underplayed her role in building the couple's wealth.) Another way to land new assignments is for cowriters to be "seen" by other talents or their representatives. As one cowriter recalled, "In terms of business, what I like ideally, [is when] I get some sort of acknowledgement from a client that I can use to secure future employment. So, for example, the fellow, the COO of [company X] gave me a very nice recommendation. It's on my Website. So . . . he's acknowledging me. And I'm able to use that to secure future business."

Overall, as long as some of their projects listed them as coauthors (or even only credited them in a book's acknowledgments), cowriters were willing to work fully undercover (i.e., invisibly) as ghostwriters on other projects. This explains why among the 62 cowriters we interviewed, 40 percent had navigated the full spectrum of recognition (from cover credit to inside acknowledgment to no public recognition) and another 40 percent had experience with two forms of recognition across their projects.[17] Assuming Jeff had only coauthored books with his name on the cover, he would definitely be an outlier—only a minority of cowriters specialized in only one form of recognition—compared to his peers.

Under such circumstances, I could understand that people denied *always* being a ghostwriter, since the nature of their projects required flexibility in their roles. The same person could sometimes be a publicly listed cowriter, other times an acknowledged "friend" or "helper," and then sometimes an undercover ghostwriter.

But in cases when people were fully and only ghostwriting—like the case of the writer I encountered during my summer travels in France—the puzzle of denying being a ghostwriter remained. It was not that he refrained from discussing his role, since he shared it, at least, with us. Nor did he seemed embarrassed to perform what others might view as stigmatized work. Instead, it seemed as if he wanted to be recognized as *more* than a ghostwriter. And based on the many other ghostwriters we subsequently interviewed, this desire of his was common.

Ghostwriters' Desires to Be Viewed as Crafters of Alternate Selves

Cowriters preferred to appear more agentic than mere invisible hired hands and talked about being crafters of alternate selves. By positioning themselves in such a way, ghostwriters highlighted their contribution to the crafting of a talent's social self, which differs from its "actual" self. The conversation I had at the summer country home captured that desire well. The famous French author's ghostwriter not only drafted the manuscripts, but he also fed the pipeline of new ideas and projects. He imagined what readers saw as a next "proper" project for the author. The ghostwriter was crafting the author's persona in more ways than I had imagined.

Granted, the ghostwriter's suggestions were proposals and the author ultimately decided what he wanted to publish under his name. Nonetheless, the ghostwriter took pride in explaining how he had crafted the persona he embodied. He recalled how he once decided, for instance, to go a bit off-track by proposing a book that appeared initially as a tangential topic for the author. "That's because I see it as reconnecting later with his roots," he noted. "Once you have written on [X] it gives you indirect credibility on [Y] and readers will want to see the parallels. That's how I convinced him to sign on." For this and many other cowriters we interviewed, capturing the talent's voice meant almost building an alternate and new character in the relationship, a character that the talent could not envision without the ghostwriter.

By animating that third character, the cowriters no longer fully disappeared into the memoir cowritten with, but publicly "by," the talent. Instead, they remained present in the altered self, which they had produced for the talent's—and the readers'—consumption. Ghostwriters explained that they not only needed to "take on [the talents'] identity," but that they also "make decisions" in "the narrative and in the dialogue and in the descriptions." This active decision-making process was the most exciting part of the project," one cowriter clarified, and the result was a "blending" of his skills with those of the talent. Consistently, most experienced cowriters presented their work as producing a voice that differed slightly from the talent's "true" voice. That is, they saw themselves as "getting into somebody's head and making them come alive on paper," but in a way that differed from real life. Thus, finding a talent's voice often meant making it "better."

Because the popular understanding of ghostwriting differs significantly from the active role that ghostwriters claim to perform, it's less surprising that they would deny being ghostwriters. From their viewpoint, they "sculpt" quotes to "create a literary character." Another ghostwriter clarified what he envisioned as a creative pursuit: "I am sort of creating—not creating a character, it's the real person—but you have to make it a good story, in a way. Because you can't—I mean, imagine how boring it would be if all we did was basically read transcripts." A third ghostwriter explained, "I used to tease [the talent]. . . . I said, 'You know, I write things that you would have said if you had thought of them.'" She added, "And, like, one time she [the talent] said, 'So you think I have a sense of humor, huh?' And I said, 'Well, you've got the one I gave you.'"

In light of their explanations, I could not help to revisit my own view of the famous French author whose "creator" I had met. What I had previously dismissed as mere idiosyncrasies in the author's radio and television persona suddenly took one a more artistic veneer. He was not only performing himself, but also a loose script that his ghostwriter had directed for him. That this particular author had been called out in the French media for some inconsistencies in his biographical presentation only lent more credibility to the way the ghost-writer depicted his work as a shaping of sort. Since the shaping did not always match reality, some close observers of the authors' work noticed the slippage between what they knew of the author's life and what was included in his books.

The shaping of an alternate self could sometimes, however, veer into creating a blueprint for a "monster," as Donald Trump's ghostwriter put it. When asked about his role advising the Hillary Clinton 2016 presidential campaign, Tony Schwartz stated that it was his "penance for having created a man who has become a monster." That is, this ghostwriter admitted to fully being part of the *creation* of something beyond the talent with whom he first worked.[18]

To deny being a ghostwriter, and, instead, to present one-self as a crafter of alternate selves: both of these phenomena are probably linked to the lingering resentment many cowrit-ers, even the more experienced ones, expressed, when asked to be fully hidden from public view. As one summed it up, "Even though these projects are not fundamentally about my ego, I have enough ego that I want the credit." They saw themselves almost as artists and longed to be recognized as such.

This craving for recognition went beyond the mere need to be seen so a new client could find them. Another person who received no recognition, explained why that concealment left them "blown away": "I mean, it's quite frankly rude to do, you know, [to] people who have worked really hard. . . . I mean, on that particular book I worked day and night. . . . There was just absolutely no acknowledgment at all. . . . It leaves you feeling very sour." To be labeled a ghostwriter only highlighted this sourness.

In another instance, a third ghostwriter expressed resentment after he was called a "hack" during a rare public appearance. He explained how he responded: "I remember once I was at a conference with a bunch of biographers, and one of the guys was a prick, and he told me, 'You shouldn't even be on this panel because you're a hack. You're a ghostwriter.' You know, and I wanted to kill him, but I kept my cool . . . There was [sic] hundreds of people in the room . . . And then I remember turning to him and asking him about the Bible. Like, 'Who wrote the Bible?' I mean we don't know. It's a kind of a holy ghostwritten book." In this case, he did not deny being a ghostwriter. Instead, he denied the interpretations and implications others were drawing from the term. Rarely were ghostwriters given such an opportunity to correct other people's misconceptions about their craft.

Denying is a form of field defense. And one of the beautiful opportunities that denying offers for interlopers is that it is a "collective endeavor" that entails "collaborative efforts."[19] For denials to take root, many people need to participate in them. Like with silencing or forgetting, this defense mechanism brings together and connects a wide group of individuals into a collective endeavor. Denials are also, therefore, bonding experiences for participants.

Take the example of ghostwriters. To deny being ghostwriters—even when fully hidden from public view—requires the collective reimagination of many cowriters (and their editors, publishers, and perhaps even talents). Even when cornered into acknowledging what they do for a living, ghostwriters often deny being ghostwriters; they might also deny the interpretations and implications of the term. Like others in circumstances in which denials are the norm, "people react as if they don't know what they know."[20] Those reactions are only possible with many others around them echoing this denial.

Within a few weeks of fieldwork, I had also internalized this shared taboo. Consequently, I switched to using the term *cowriter*, so as to signal my complicity with them. Never again, except in academic publications, did I refer to the term *ghostwriter*.

Besides creating bonding experiences, denials can also prove a versatile defense mechanism. As hinted above, many varied elements can sequentially or simultaneously be denied. In his typology of denials, the sociologist Stanley Cohen makes clear the extent of possible denial combinations. As he writes, people can engage in "literal," "interpretative," or "implicatory" forms of denials.[21] (NB: The implicatory form amounts to denying consequences.) Moreover, denials can be conscious or not, operate at multiple levels (e.g., personal, cultural, and official), concern historical or contemporary elements, and be voiced by victims, perpetrators, and observers. The versatility of denials seems almost endless and, as such, calls for layered meanings.

In the publishing industry, the multiparty complicity between ghostwriters, talents, and others—complicity, that is, in denying that a ghostwriter was part of a book project—suggests this versatility and layering of denial. Ghostwriters do not want to be seen as such because of the interpretive association that observers imbue the term with (e.g., cowriters only transcribe what the talent dictates and have little role in shaping the persona). In parallel, talents do not want to admit using a ghostwriter, for fear of the implications of such an admission: they might be denied their roles as "authors," even if they contribute little more than orally answering a cowriter's queries; and readers might suspect the text is not authentic enough, since it was ghostwritten.

Together, all parties involved coalesce to deny, repeatedly yet differently, the very existence of ghostwriters. In more complex situations, the flavors and layering can increase exponentially and create a complex web of cultural scaffolds, worthy of exploration. Denials can point to more than stigmatization. Here, they unearthed ghostwriters' deep desire for recognition and for the opportunity to reimagine themselves on their own terms.

Denying's Implications for Interlopers

First, I suspect that, in their field pursuits, interlopers encounter denials less often than other defense mechanisms (such as silencing and obstructing). The fact that denials are very difficult to reverse once they are set in motion might account for this low frequency of occurrence. While a field can suddenly decide to "open" access to someone it previously obstructed, or an organization can suddenly "remember" what it once forgot, turning around after a denial is trickier. That's why many fields and organizations tend not to deny too often, or in too precise terms, what interlopers believe might be happening inside these settings. (Only when cornered do people usually deny something.)

When the line of defense breaks after a denial, debacles can easily ensue. The following example illustrates such a debacle, a consequence of what many perceived as a denial. When the Paris Institute of Political Studies was recently confronted with incest allegations against one of its key faculty members, the school's director publicly announced that he was shocked by such revelations. He also suggested that he had not been aware of them prior to their recent discovery, implicitly denying that he had prior knowledge of them and brushing them off, instead, as rumors. A few weeks later, however, it emerged that he had personally informed one of the highest-ranking French government officials of these allegations, two years prior to his supposed "shock."

The director's initial implicit denial swiftly became indefensible; consequently, he resigned from the school's directorship, amid pressure from the press, students, and some school members. A governmental commission was set up to investigate the director's handling of the crisis. Most people interviewed by the commission reported that they perceived his behavior as amounting to "a lie, and not only an error by omission, since the director opted to keep quiet what he knew during his first communication [on the topic]."[22]

Second, denials seem like sturdy defenses. And yet, they are more delicate and fragile than it appears. Even when interlopers face denials, the chances for slippages usually offer opportunities for them to forge a pathway through the defense. As suggested earlier, a constant and widespread (re)socialization of field participants is often required to sustain denials. In the freelance ghostwriting world, for instance, the regular entry of new aspiring cowriters calls for repeated socialization. Rookies might not fully grasp what "cowriting" really entails and be content with simply transcribing (rather than shaping) a talent's words. In doing so, they might lend credence to the idea that they have little agency. By contrast, most experienced cowriters frown upon the notion that they are mere "stenographers." Also, depending on the scope and duration of elements being denied, the number of those involved can rise quickly. In many instances (such as genocides), the denials crumble, in part because of the sheer number and continued involvement of participants.

In addition, well-informed interlopers who feel they are being lied to can become fierce advocates for what they see as a more truthful depiction of reality. Thus, instead of dampening their inquiries, denials can fuel their desire to make their points and breach the defenses. This can lead interlopers, in some cases, to engage in even more "daring" or "suicidal" attempts to convince others. Such behavior on the part of interlopers is probably facilitated by the growing isolation they might feel. As the psychologist William Kahn remarks, "The more that people side with denial—with mandated blindness, deafness, and muteness—the more isolated and at risk are others wishing to speak the truth of what they see, think, and feel."[23]

Isolated individuals have little to lose and can become quite fearless. Fearless individuals become loose elements, difficult to tame or control. Again, I speak in part from experience.

When studying the moral undertones of faculty socialization at the Harvard Business School (see chapter 5), several school insiders pushed back against my project, with layered denials. A first form of denial centered on the school not having any specific moral agenda (literally denying the issue of the inquiry itself). A second form of denial posited that, even if the school did have a moral agenda, my interpretation of that agenda was erroneous because I did not have the full picture of the internal dynamics. A third form of denial entailed admitting that the school might have a moral agenda and that my description of it as an ideology of non-ideology might encapsulate it correctly; and yet, this third denial asserted that studying these dynamics did not really matter, since the school's societal role was less important than it appeared (implicatory denial). This was the only time any school member told me HBS was irrelevant!

The more I listened to these arguments, the more I coded them as denials and the more intent I became on proving them wrong. A few months after joining my new employer (Boston University), a colleague who had partly managed my hiring

case told me in passing that he had dubbed the resulting ethnography I had published on HBS (and that he had reviewed)
a "death wish." My perceived reckless behavior by pursuing my
research project indicated, in his eyes, that I wanted to sym-
bolically "die" in the hands of my previous employer. I suspect
he was exaggerating a bit my inner thought process. But he did
have a point, which might prove common among interlopers
faced with denials. Denials simply fuel our desire to continue
digging deeper and make us even more tenacious in our
quests.

Conclusion

FIELD ACCESS IS often touted as the sine qua non condition for fieldworkers to engage in their pursuits. Without access, they are seen as lonely bystanders to the imagined action inside the field. They are mere lurkers, behind a glass window, who are forbidden from partaking in the fun. That's why "a problem that afflicts almost all researchers—at least all those who attempt to study, by whatever method, organizations, groups, and communities in the real world—is getting in."[1] The assumption is that understanding a setting and its inner working is doomed without proper access. Yet the process itself of trying to access a field—regardless of outcomes—is more telling than generally recognized.

In this book, I have argued that the defenses that interlopers face contain way more analytical possibilities than most fieldworkers imagine. Whether an interloper's attempts to inquire into an issue are denied, forgotten, or silenced can prove indicative of key tensions within a field. Also, the manner in which an attempt is obstructed, an issue of concern is shelved, or field elements are hidden from an interloper's view can be suggestive of other participants' main challenges. Thus, when faced with repeated defenses, interlopers can follow new alleys of discovery that they could hardly have imagined upfront. What might we lose by treating these annoyances as mere afterthoughts? A lot, I would argue, and perhaps even the seeds of the discovery process itself.[2]

If field defenses are solutions that people develop to solve challenges they face together, then analyzing them offers deep insights into these challenges. Field defenses are generative moments and often occasions for developing understandings.[3] "If a respondent is annoyed or resistant," we need to "listen to their concerns," notes the sociologist Annette Lareau.[4] Many of the examples presented in this book illustrate how defenses play out differently across fields and reflect their unique circumstances. Those differences and their uniqueness require our full and sustained attention.

Instead of brushing aside the hurdles we face, we need to better grapple with them.[5] As Rabinow reminds us, "The constant breakdown [in fieldwork] . . . is not just an annoying accident but a core aspect of this type of inquiry."[6] I will be the first to admit that it is sometimes hard to know whether a breakdown is simply a technical glitch or a true sign of more to come. As the sociologist Jennifer Croissant notes, when we face uncertainties in our inquiries, it can be because something is yet to be solved or is endemic to a given field.[7] Since we cannot *a priori* know what might end up being endemic, we need to remain constantly alert. While defenses alone cannot illuminate a field, they do often provide strong signals about what might lurk below.

Tellingly, not all fields can adopt all defenses. Conditions of their use vary, and the adoption of one line of defense versus another already points to how a field might be structured. For example, fields with high turnover among their members might be better off relying on obstructing, hiding, and shelving (contained defense efforts by select individuals in reaction to given intrusions) than forgetting, silencing, and denying (which require constant resocialization of all members). Relatedly, fields that rely more heavily on internally focused defenses or ones aimed at controlling their members (such as silencing and shelving) might lack the social cohesion that is commonly found in settings more likely to deploy more outwardly focused defenses or ones geared towards preventing outside scrutiny (such as obstructing and denying). Those propositions are meant simply to provide some guideposts on the particularities of each discussed line of defense. More systematic analysis of these and other particularities of each defense is, of course, needed.

Finally, in the same way that forms of resistance upon entry prove analytically helpful, other forms of field reactivity might lend themselves to similar inquiry. Such reactivity can include field participants' up-front unique embrace of a researcher and their specific reactions to this person's exit from the field. An overly welcoming embrace should make any fieldworker pause: it could, for instance, signal a form of proselytism worth exploring or a desire to transform new members.[8] But do field participants embrace you specifically, or anyone who approaches them? Is their embrace continuous or simply temporary? Answers to such questions can teach us a lot about a field.

Also, as the ethnographer John Van Maanen remarks, the process of leaving a field is rarely discussed yet also critical.[9] I suspect that analyzing forms of exit can prove as insightful as analyzing access. Do field participants suddenly stop inviting you to their gatherings and remove you from their communications (including unfriending you on social media) as a sort of expedite exit? Could they pretend instead that you simply never were part of their community? Or do they slowly wean you from the field? Each of these forms of exit might prove illuminating.

I would be remiss, however, to leave the impression that accessing (or exiting) a field entails only challenges, problems, and slammed doors for interlopers. What makes any efforts worthwhile are the "highs" that interlopers get from their journeys. The matching of interlopers and their fields is generally littered with uneasy turns and missteps. Yet the many denials, silences, and other defense mechanisms they encounter also offer a glimpse of what makes interlopers thrive. Engaging in field research can be frustrating at times but also has the potential to be exciting. Without the excitement, or what could be labeled as highs, none of us would continue pursuing fieldwork.

Most field researchers develop, with practice, their own more precise definition of what codes as a field high. These instances are intimately linked to our trajectories and what we bring to our fields. Not all settings can offer the preferred highs, and finding them requires trial and error. Beyond my fluency in identifying and juggling field defenses (see coda), the pleasure I find in seeing defenses melt down probably explains my pull towards hard-to-access fields.[10] In these settings, I feel perhaps most agential and useful as a person—in other words, alive. Like criminals who get seduced by committing crimes, the distinctive attraction derived from seeing barriers tumble are likely part of the motivation for many of my research pursuits.[11]

Other field researchers undoubtfully thrive on different highs. The varieties of field highs are almost endless.[12] For some field researchers, the excitement might come from being embraced by other field participants when observing them at their homes.[13] For others, the joy might come from finally being covertly hired in the setting they hope to study.[14] Yet others might become animated in response to witnessing mistakes and crises and deciphering how and why people make sense of how things go wrong.[15] We rarely spotlight the highs that certain kinds of fieldwork, or for that matter other research designs, offer us.[16] But without them, we would simply move on.

When fieldworkers fail to become interlopers, a lot can be lost. It's only by inquiring into a variety of settings than we can gain a more universal understanding of the broader world. Doing so requires the training, deployment, and persistence of an army of interlopers across settings and times, with the hope of learning ever more about social worlds. Doing so also calls for pushing the boundaries and persisting when faced with apparent hurdles.[17]

If we only opt for settings that welcome us, we simply don't know what dynamics we might be missing. The rich ecology of storytelling that fieldworkers can help construct then becomes highjacked by powerful field participants who dictate a singular reading of their worlds.[18] Without us interfering, these participants can easily perpetuate narratives that often prove self-serving. Moreover, if only pursuing easily accessible fields, we remain in the dark about the possibly inaccurate generalizations we might be drawing from them. I hope that we all try harder to study fields where data seem difficult to collect rather than focus on those easiest to access.

The meddling that we typically associate with interlopers might not be the only way to conduct field research and develop new knowledge. It remains nonetheless one of the most widespread pathways into fields. Interlopers might therefore seem a bit groundbreaking in their field behavior, but they are actually following a traditional and time-tested route— one that has led many others to face seemingly endless resistance and, often unknowingly, learn from these defenses more than initially meets the eye. The only pathway forward is therefore onward.

Coda

MOST OF THIS BOOK has focused on field access and field
defense mechanisms without paying too much attention to
interlopers' unique roles in recognizing or even prompting
such defenses. Yet fieldwork is an interactive pursuit that
entails an embodied person attempting to better understand a
given field.[1] In those moments, the researchers' experiences
become a "social spring and vector of knowledge" that informs
the inquiry.[2] The back-and-forth that fieldworkers engage in
with a field also reflects an older and less obvious adventure—
both for the field and the interloper in question—that requires
more consideration.

Accessing a field is what crowns the collaborative journey
already taken (at least in part), rather than generating a
moment of sudden reckoning. In that sense, field participants'
reactions not only teach us something about a field, but also
about fieldworkers themselves.[3] In her moving essay on the
social psychologist Philip Brickman's life (who studied happiness
and ended his life by suicide), the journalist Jennifer Senior
tellingly notes that "we all find ways to study ourselves."[4] I agree

and would only add that we all find ways to study *one version* of ourselves—a bit like the third, crafted self in the cowriter/ author relationship (see chapter 6).

At the "receiving" end of field defenses, interlopers—with their own histories and questions—filter the field's reactions and build objects of study that, in retrospect, look way more "polished" than they initially were. More specifically, field- workers put their "own organism, sensibility, and incarnate intelligence at the epicenter" of the field context they intend to dissect.[5] Their feelings, sensations, and emotions form as many points of contact as their initial research designs. The ensuing dance is idiosyncratic, based on the unique combina- tion of a given interloper and specific field defenses.[6]

Interlopers always bring with them some knowledge of pre- viously acquired steps that they try to insert into the dance. Those steps are inherently linked to versions of ourselves that we carry into new field experiences and that are taken from previous ones. The versions of ourselves are of course multidi- mensional and dynamic; making it hard to pinpoint any sin- gular one as informing an inquiry. Some version, nonetheless, seems salient and robust enough over time to accompany us from field to field. Gaining clearer awareness of the interplay between those versions and the fieldwork being conducted helps contextualize the match between an embodied researcher and a given inquiry.

I suspect that many researchers can point to unique affini- ties between their objects of study and their own trajectories.[7] Since I am less familiar with their stories, I will use my own to try and explain how my acquired "steps" might have shaped my field relations and, ultimately, the dances that I pursued. If any- thing, the "explanation" I will provide might help justify, at least to myself, and excuse for others, my occasional stubbornness when dealing with field defenses. More importantly, it might help explain both my familiarity with and interest in melting down field defenses.

The version of myself that I believe informs my research on field defenses is best captured in a memory I have of attending, several years back, a bat mitzvah party in Boston. The bat mitzvah girls were daughters of family friends; their parents had known my parents as well as my late grandparents for decades. These friends treated me almost as an extended family member. During the dinner celebration, all the guests had been seated at prearranged tables in an effort to mix people up and create a festive atmosphere. I sat with my spouse at a table slightly out of view from the front of the room but still within the "core" circles of family friends. More distant acquaintances and youth were seated in the circles further out.

When the time came during the party to have guests share a few words, our family friends surprised a series of attendees they considered family members or close friends, by calling on them to say a few words. The married and even unwed couples were always called in pairs. They were then ushered up to the room's center to offer some words of advice or congratulations. After several iterations of couples stepping up, I heard my name called out. I was also stunned when it was *not* followed by my spouse's name. While he was not as close to the family as I was, he had met them several times, had been nominally invited to the festivities (i.e., the invitation bore both our names), and had been seated next to me. And yet, in this moment, many familiar defense mechanisms suddenly kicked in. The same-sex nature of my relationship apparently rendered our couple best left unrecognized.

I recall my huge discomfort in hearing only my name. The other couple seated at our table, whom we knew, also looked at us in disbelief. My spouse's face was livid. I felt stranded and transported back to an earlier and more painful period in my life. I walked slowly to the center of the room and said very brief words before retreating to my seat.

I know I should have grabbed my spouse and asked him to accompany me. Yet I went with the defensive illusion that I was single, all too aware that I had seen such denials before and become numb to their violence. I cannot hold these family friends solely accountable. They likely channeled the dynamics that they had seen exhibited in my own family. Crucially, this moment crystallized more layers of defenses in just one split second than ever before: it captured an ability to deny what was clearly known, to silence what should not be uttered, and to hide someone in plain sight.

This episode is relevant because it also points to my acquired "skill" of noticing and dealing with—in this case, deflecting—such defenses. The parallels between my early socialization and my attraction to studying hard-to-access fields and their defense mechanisms are likely not coinciden-tal.[8] Families can be fertile training grounds for aspiring field-workers. They offer the holding environment to develop their interests and aspirations. They also provide, even often unbe-knownst to those involved, the basis for fieldworkers' future trajectories. I cannot therefore stress enough the developmen-tal role that my close and extended family members have played in helping me get where I am. Without their combined years of attention, nurturing concern, and avid listening, I would likely still be puddling around aimlessly.

At the same time, if doing "fieldwork apparently requires some of the instincts of an exile,"[9] then identifying as gay in a seemingly straight family is sure to provide good training grounds for those instincts. The anthropologist Michael Agar posited that some researchers develop an affinity with ethnography because, among other reasons, it either "justifies their detachment from what others consider important" or "justifies an interest in exploring different lifeways."[10] These reasons resonate with my experience growing up feeling "different" from others around me.

That difference, as I slowly learned, was more relative than I imagined, and more the result of layered defense mechanisms in my close family than completely objective. Critically, these defenses also taught me a lot about how my family dealt with tension, which was unknown to me until then. Denials, silencing, and more were all ways to handle these "challenges." Thus, it's not fully surprising, in retrospect, that my close family initially reacted the way it did. Nor was it surprising that I ended up being attracted to studying varieties of field defenses.

While deciphering my sexual orientation took some time for me to sort out, my awareness of being a budding social scientist was probably more affirmed. I clearly recall the day when I walked into a bookstore to purchase two magazines: one was *Playboy*, the other *Playgirl*. (Gay magazines were less common in mainstream bookstores at the time and the floodgates of online exploration had not yet opened.) Given my (then) youngish looks or the incongruity of my purchases, I got carded by the clerk. Upon showing my driver's license, the clerk rang up my purchases. Once past that slightly embarrassing moment, I walked out rather pleased with myself to have devised such an impartial way to sort out any confusion. The controlled experiment proved conclusive, and over time I gradually grew more comfortable with being attracted to men.

The same could not be said of my family. Like in many other French families in the 1990s, acknowledging harboring a gay son was, I suspect, not an easy step. Both my parents came from Jewish households with seemingly little experience with sexual minorities. The defense mechanisms deployed shortly after my coming out surprised me, however, by their strength and endless variety. The first salvo of defense came in the form of a denial. Of course people experiment at various stages of their lives, but ultimately marrying a woman was on my horizon, or at least that was the general narrative put forth by some family members. Perhaps they were partly right: marrying seemed possible, marrying an opposite-sex partner much less so at the time.[11]

Rapidly, after the limited results of the denials, hiding and silencing became the new norm for dealing with homosexuality in my immediate family. For instance, many pictures of my graduation seem to inadvertently omit my partner (not yet spouse), who was always in attendance. Had he been a she, would he have been included in more pictures? By then, it was hard for me to know, since my "controlled experiments" had halted. Still, years later and in other instances, when my parents' acquaintances would ask them whether I was married, their typical answer was no, without any further explanation. This silence probably protected them, since defenses can ease anxieties.[12] But my parents' reaction was likely also sharpened by a family history that I gradually discovered.

With time, some family "secrets" were revealed. I learned that many events that involved same-sex behavior in my family had long been hidden. The first revelation centered on a close and older cousin that I saw frequently who had divorced his wife yet often went on vacation with her, their kids, and her new husband. That holiday configuration (i.e., what seemed like a ménage à trois) had often struck me—even as a child—as odd, but it suddenly made sense when the cousin came out as gay and mentioned it as a reason for ending his marriage. The fact that he had been married and had children prior to his coming out also shed light on my parent's initial denial: here was a "model" of a gay man married to a straight woman with children.

In addition to this first revelation, I learned a few years later that another older cousin—generally described elusively as "troubled" in the rare instances his name came up at gatherings—had been molested as a youth by his male coach. After that, he received what was referred to in the 1960s as "therapy" and never really recovered. The cousin lived somewhat hidden from view before passing away, providing yet another family model of a possible way to deal with male homosexuality. I recall visiting his mother and sister's home more than once as a child and always wondering where he was. Both relatives were as tight-lipped as ever during my visits and rarely uttered a word about him, except to steer the conversation away as fast as they could. These episodes taught me yet another way people could mount defenses by hiding and silencing interlopers.

It runs in the family! By "it," this older relative meant homosexuality. She was the person I was closest to from her generation, and she was not shy about adding pieces to the puzzle. As I recounted the above discoveries to her, she seemed unfazed. She had heard talk of my great uncle's rumored same-sex attraction. *Apples don't fall far from the tree*, she added, to provide context to what she noticed. And to boost her claim, she pointed to the numerous cousins—a generation below me—who also came out a decade or so after me. Considering such a history, the barrage of defenses against homosexuality that I experienced suddenly took on a new meaning. These reactions built on a particular family dynamic. They reflected multigenerational concerns, and well-learned ways—defenses—to assuage them.

In sharing these biographical elements, my aim is to spotlight what might have rendered me uniquely attuned to decrypting field defense mechanisms. Above and beyond any "queer" or outsider sensibility of persisting in the face of resistance, my own family's historical dynamics prepared me well to tackle these defenses.[13] I trust there are many more reasons, so I don't want to oversimplify the match between an interloper and a field.[14] Nonetheless, I hope these insights start to illuminate such matches and many others.

Ultimately, fields are only what we make of them. All fieldworkers stepping into new or known contexts carry with them the seeds that will nourish and fuel the interactions to come. When field participants defend themselves, they signal not only what matters to them but also what kind of dance interlopers might be good at picking up on. The notion of a fieldworker being adopted by a field is probably more literal than we imagine.

ACKNOWLEDGMENTS

I AM GRATEFUL to the many and interlocking research communities that have sustained me over the years. I first publicly voiced the kernel of this book's idea during an annual "May Meaning Meeting" hosted by Amy Wrzesniewski and Michael Pratt that brought together faculty and doctoral students from several universities. Amy has often seen threads in my work that I rarely discern. During a presentation, after explaining that I was interviewing ghostwriters, I joked that it probably was an obvious next research setting given that I had already studied forgetting, silencing, and invisibility dynamics. Sue Ashford teased me that this combination required more probing. I am ever thankful to her comment and the seed she helped plant that day.

Around the same time, Kim Elsbach and Rod Kramer offered me an opportunity to write a short essay for a handbook on qualitative methodologies that they were editing. I titled my essay "Denials, Obstructions, and Silences: Lessons from Field Resistance (and Field Embrace)" and it encouraged me to want to continue examining these issues. Its very short format left me wanting to do much more. But again, the opportunity they provided me to sketch out my initial thoughts was very inspiring.

Since then, ongoing conversations with many colleagues have helped me sharpen my argument. I thank the Boston Field Research Conference participants and the Boston University's Precarity Lab members for their feedback and collective wisdom. Also, separate conversations with my colleagues Nishani Bourmault, Mary Ann Glynn, Alya Guseva, and Ashley

Mears proved very helpful in clarifying my thoughts. Critically, late night discussion with Beth Bechky, Christine Beckman, Melissa Mazmanian, Siobhán O'Mahony, Gerardo Okhuysen, and Mark Zbaracki provided the nurturing environment that allowed me to embark on this project.

I cannot thank enough my collaborators in the various field projects I discuss in the book. Their companionship and insights have made my fieldwork experiences less solitary and much more enjoyable. They also shaped this book in more ways than I can ever acknowledge. I am tremendously grateful to Curtis Chan, Bella Fong, Virág Molnár, Audrey Holm, and Nicholas Occhiuto for putting up with me in these meandering adventures. Working alongside such a talented group of people is a real treat.

I also thank for their combined guidance the many insightful editors and reviewers of the articles that came out of the above inquiries. Their spirits infuse the current chapters. Some materials for chapter 1 appeared in *Administrative Science Quarterly* as "Markets, Morals, and Practices of Trade: Jurisdictional Disputes in the U.S. Commerce in Cadavers" (2010), for chapter 2 in *Organization Science* as "A Self-Fulfilling Cycle of Coercive Surveillance: Workers' Invisibility Practices and Managerial Justification" (2018), for chapter 4 in *Research in the Sociology of Organizations* as "The Ideology of Silence at the Harvard Business School: Structuring Faculty's Teaching Tasks for Moral Relativism" (2016), for chapter 5 in *Academy of Management Journal* as "Collective Memory Meets Organizational Identity: Remembering to Forget in a Firm's Rhetorical History" (2012), and for chapter 6 in *Social Forces* as "Stand-In Labor and the Rising Economy of Self" (2020).

I am immensely thankful to those who provided feedback on the manuscript. Ben Platt's editorial suggestions on an initial draft of it proved invaluable. Not only is he a joy to work with but his remarkably gentle yet pointed guidance proved ideal to help me move forward. I cannot imagine a better reader and midwife for this project. Alongside his assistance, Bella Fong's initial and Sara Snitselaar's later reading of the full manuscript as well as Valerio Iannucci's comments on parts of the manuscript were also very useful. I also feel very lucky to have benefited from Carolyn Elerding's close reading of this book. Her insights and careful attention to, among other things, gender and power dynamics proved key in strengthening the text. Finally, I thank Tobias Ryan and Jaden Young for proofreading the manuscript and Beth Nauman-Montana for indexing it.

At Princeton University Press, Meagan Levinson's unwavering support for this project proved critical. It was a pleasure to work with someone who immediately got what the book was about and helped me shape it in that manner. Her last editorial suggestions were also spot on. Furthermore, she was able to secure three thoughtful reviewers who ultimately made this book a better one. I am grateful for the time they collectively invested in reading the manuscript and for their numerous suggestions. Rene Almeling and Stefan Timmermans proved particularly instrumental in getting this book into print; many thanks to them.

Drafting this book would not have been possible without a sabbatical from Boston University's Questrom School of Business, a visiting fellowship at the Max Planck Sciences Po (MaxPo) Center in Paris, and a short visit at Sciences Po's Center for the Sociology of Organizations (CSO). Amid an ever-evolving pandemic, the MaxPo Center provided me with a haven of peace and stability that allowed me to write a first draft of this book in spring 2021. I am indebted to Olivier Godechot and Cornelia Woll for inviting me into their community. The wall clock in the visitor's office where I stayed was conveniently stalled at 2:35 p.m., giving me the false impression that I had endless time to write. I would encourage them to consider never repairing it! Also, at the CSO, Sophie Dubuisson-Quellier and Patrick Castel graciously hosted me for a few short weeks to finalize this draft.

Finally, my family, past and present, has its imprint all over this work. I am grateful to my father, aunt, and uncle for showing me how love and resistance could mesh so effortlessly; to my sister and cousins for showcasing the endless possibilities of reinvention, generation after generation; and to my mother for providing a role model for diving fearlessly into new worlds. She has, as of now, relocated to an entirely new country three times and was always able, each time, to carve out a place in these worlds to sustain her. For all I know, she might be the ultimate interloper.

As always, my deepest gratitude goes to Patrick, who strongly encouraged me to write this book. When I hesitated about committing to the project, he ceaselessly reminded me that it reflected who I was and needed to be written. He even commented on it in a language that is not his own. It's only fitting therefore to end in his native language: *mille mercis*, a thousand thanks! You always inspire me to do more than I can imagine and in ways for which I am forever grateful.

NOTES

Introduction

1. Field participants commonly test researchers to vet them before opening access. Such a process can even entail a "series of tests" as Robert McNamara (1994, 9) explains in his study of New York City Time Square hustlers. Hustlers would provide him information to "be held in strict confidence" and see whether he shared it with others. They would also try to extort cash from him despite his claim that he would never pay his interviewees. Only after passing all these tests did they open up to him. In other contexts, the tests can be much more instantaneous and decisive. When Elijah Anderson (1989) tried to learn more about the community that was hanging out at Jelly's bar and liquor store in the South Side of Chicago, it took him a while to figure out how to blend in. After one regular chatted him up over drinks one day and asked him what he was doing: Anderson explained he was a graduate student. That answer showed he was the "right kind of people" (15) to hang out with, because he seemed steadily employed and with family ties, unlike the "wineheads" (there only for the wine and fun) and "hoodlums" (those who cared about being tough and getting big money) that regulars avoided.

2. A corollary of the bliss and excitement that many fieldworkers experience after gaining access is the informal "debt" now owed to gatekeepers; see (Gibson-Light and Seim 2020, 676).

3. Rabinow 1977, 80.

4. Gary Alan Fine (2007, xi), for example, who tried to study meteorologists, recalls nervously going to meet a key gatekeeper who "had the fate of my [his] research in his hands." Upon hearing from this person "When do you want to start?" all Fine's anxiety dissipated.

5. Upon spending an inordinate amount of time trying to study the publishing industry—by alternating between a "foot in the door" and "door in the face" technique—and growing more desperate by the day, Clayton Childress's luck suddenly turned around when he found a publisher willing to introduce him to an author (Childress 2017, 247). (The former technique aims at getting a person to agree to a large request by having them agree to a modest one first. The latter technique aims at convincing a person to comply by making a large request that they most likely will turn down, before presenting a more modest one.)

6. Feldman, Bell, and Berger 2004.

7. Harrington 2003.

8. Other writings on gaining access include articles such as "Exchange and Access in Field Work" (Gray 1980) and the book section titled "Gaining Entry" from *In the Field: Reading on the Field Research Experience* (Smith and Kornblum 1996).

9. Vaughan 2021, 18.

10. See Jack Katz's (1982) discussion of reactivity and access in the field for more details. As he explains, the question of access is not merely one at the start of the study, but also an "ongoing" negotiation "continued from situation to situation" and "from the beginning to the end" of the inquiry (208).

11. Feldman, Bell, and Berger 2004, ix.

12. Whether it be women seeking the official right to vote (Banaszak 1996), French chefs trying to promote a new cuisine (Rao, Monin, and Durand 2003), or individuals trying to challenge corporations (King and Pearce 2010), advocates of any given issue face comparable field resistance.

13. See Rene Almeling's (2020) insightful discussion on the production of "non-knowledge" in relation to the missing science of men's reproductive health, and Jennifer Croissant's (2014) illuminating review article on agnotology or the study of culturally induced ignorance.

14. Consider Diane Vaughan's (1996) study of the Challenger launch disaster, Mark Zbaracki and Mark Bergen's (2010) inquiry into price adjustments in a manufacturing firm, Mark de Rond's (2017) examination of British military doctors' work in Afghanistan, and Irene Padavic, Robin Ely, and Erin Reid's (2020) deep dive into a consulting firm's culture: all were invited into the field to conduct their research by key participants.

15. Cases of insiders studying their own settings abound. For instance, Matthew Desmond (2007) was a firefighter prior to conducting his examination of firefighting; Karen Ho (2009), Callen Anthony (2021), and Alexandra Michel (2023) were all bankers before looking into Wall Street bankers' lives; Leslie Perlow (2012) was a consultant prior to studying their relationship to time, and Michèle Lamont (2009) and Christine Musselin (2022) were both professors prior to studying academic dynamics.

16. It's not surprising that the sociologist Everett Hughes uses the term "double agent" when referring to field-workers, to capture the possibility that anyone can turn on someone else (1974).

17. The more "protected" the setting, the higher the likelihood of field resistance. Scholars studying prisons and courts are perhaps the ones dealing with the most resistance (e.g., Clair 2020; Gibson-Light and Seim 2020; Simes, Western, and Lee 2022). Other scholars studying illegitimate activities also expect resistance (e.g., Beckert and Dewey 2017; Hudson and Okhuysen 2009; Toubiana and Ruebottom 2022). But, more generally, anyone studying people in positions of power or belonging to marginalized groups should expect resistance. As Bruno Cousin, Shamus Khan, and Ashley Mears (2018) remind us about elites, "unlike the majority of other groups, elites generally confront researchers with greater resources, such as legal and institutional power" (238). And as Kathleen Gerson

and Sarah Damaske (2020) note, "members of marginalized groups, who are more likely—and rightly so—to perceive a wide social distance separating them from any researcher, may harbor especially strong suspicions [vis-à-vis researchers]" (122).

18. I don't want to give the false impression, however, that I unknowingly got derailed in these projects. Instead, I often relish these challenges and run head-first, even proactively, into hard-to-access fields. The defenses they mount are ones that seem quite familiar to me for reasons that I will explain in the coda, and ones that I have known almost intuitively how to grapple with, even if not always successfully.

19. Rachel Sherman (2019) offers perhaps my favorite example of finding an alternate entry into a field. When her efforts to interview wealthy New Yorkers fizzled, she noticed that many of them had recently conducted major home renovations. Thus, her sampling strategy shifted to focus on people who had done such renovations (243).

20. Rabinow 1977, 87.

21. Morrill 1995, 2.

22. Cited by Turco 2016, 66.

23. Journalists often exploit the suggestion of guilt coming from an absence of a response when reporting that they reached out several times for comments to person and that none were provided.

24. I am indebted to Calvin Morrill, Mayer N. Zald, and Hayagreeva Rao (2003) for piquing my interest in covert activities. While their notion of covert political conflict shares with my notion of covert field defense the idea that they are both "simmering beneath the surface" (392), they view that form of conflict as emerging *from below*, whereas I view the form of defense as emerging both *from above and below* (i.e., implicating all field participants regardless of their place in the field hierarchy).

25. Anna Freud (1966) offers the seminal definition of individual defense mechanisms. She conceptualizes them as unconscious strategies by which people distort or deny reality to defend themselves against the experience of anxiety. I mostly agree with this definition but refrain from qualifying a field defense as unconscious.

26. I realize that this inside-outside divide is somewhat of an oversimplification and contains many layered dynamics beyond what is implied here. For more details on the porosity of this divide, see Nancy Naples (1996).

27. Examples of a more overt forms of field resistance could be an official communication from a government agency declining to participate in a research project, and a reply from a CEO stating that his firm is not interested in supporting a research endeavor.

28. While I present each defense separately, it's obvious that defenses can be deployed in complementary ways; thus, any field or organization can exhibit layers of combined defenses that might prove hard to disentangle.

29. See Iskander 2021, 274; Gibson-Light and Seim 2020, 685; Harrington 2016, 24 for examples of a fieldworker suddenly deemed no longer legally

"compliant," or threatened with legal sanctions. See Hooker (1993) and Verdery (2018) for instances of fieldworkers put under constant, intensive surveillance. See Hanson and Richards (2019) for accounts of fieldworkers being sexually harassed.

30. In interviews, the resistance that interviewees put forward has long been noted. Howard Becker and Blanche Geer remark: "Frequently, people do not tell an interviewer all the things he might want to know. This may be because they do not want to, feeling that to speak of some particular subject would be impolitic, impolite, or insensitive, because they do not think to and because the interviewer does not have enough information to inquire into the matter, or because they are not able to. The first case—the problem of 'resistance'—is well known and a considerable lore has developed about how to cope with it." (1957, 30). They write about coping with resistance, not however about analyzing it. More recently, Kathleen Gerson and Sarah Damaske (2020) note in their book *The Science and Art of Interviewing* that "it is no surprise that people of all stripes are more likely than ever to greet an interviewer's request with skepticism and resistance" (122). But again, the focus is more on overcoming than analyzing resistance.

31. Many scholars have discussed "field reactivity" and offered suggestions on how to handle it (e.g., Bernstein 2012, 188; Katz 1982, 208; Lamont 2009, 254; Warikoo 2016, 213).

32. Gatekeepers are widely studied in cultural fields (Childress 2017; Godart, Hsu, and Negro 2023; Godart and Mears 2009; Hamann and Beljean 2021; Hirsch 1972). They are the ones patrolling a unique cultural "taste" and deploying its associated justifying narrative. In corporations, the public relations staff obviously play a similar role. But many other fields also harbor their own gatekeepers.

33. For a discussion of how to assess any given story see Small and Calarco (2022), and for a more specific discussion of the "interpretative" validity of ethnographic research see Evans, Huising, and Silbey (2015).

34. As Jennifer Croissant (2014) rightfully points out, not *all* forms of resistance (such as the case of ignorance that she considers) produce "yet-to-be-known" knowledge: "The epistemological relationality of ignorance is closely paralleled by but not identical to the issues of time in assessing knowledge and agnosis. If the epistemology of ignorance is in part locative in terms of spaces (metaphoric social spaces, literal geographies), then time needs to be figured carefully in discussions of ignorance, as there are forms of agnosis which figure as the not-yet-known, and others as the forgotten or obliterated" (8).

35. Brown-Saracino 2014, 43.

36. Darmon 2005, 112; author's translation.

37. See Diane Vaughan (1996) for an example of an apparently odd field phenomena (i.e., normalizing deviance) being a routine product rather than a by-product of the field.

38. Katherine Kellogg (2011) offers a notable example of a fieldworker adopting participants' habits. When studying a reform in surgery departments, she noticed that ultimately, residents "seemed to be choosing sides in a fight." But, initially, residents did not pick sides. Instead, she reports, "they did their work and kept their mouth shut, and I did the same" (15). Doing as they did allowed her to blend in.

NOTES [161]

39. Goffman 1989, 129.

40. Cited by Noiriel 1990, 147; author's translation.

41. For a more in-depth discussion of reflexivity in qualitative research designs see Alvesson and Sköldberg (2018); Bourdieu and Wacquant (1992).

42. Van Maanen 2011.

43. Barley 2004.

44. There is a clear difference between studying settings at the margins and being typecast by mainstream readers as being (as a scholar) "at the margins" of academia. In my view, research *from* the margins can build knowledge about the mainstream viewpoint and therefore is not positioned *at* the margins.

45. Barley 2004, 69.

46. Harrington 2003, 618–19.

47. My interest in overcoming defenses fits well with Amy L. Stone's (2018) notion of acquired "queer persistence" defined as "relentlessly following leads, researching in unexpected places, and pushing past self-doubt" (221). Such a persistent stance echoes the broader mandate of a "queer methodological approach" aiming to clarify, but not overdetermine, the conditions that make life livable for individuals (including for fieldworkers). This mandate is spelled out in more details by Matt Brim and Amin Ghaziani (2016, 19) and D'Lane Compton, Tey Meadow and Kristen Schilt (2018, 7). See also Nancy Rothbard and Lakshmi Ramarajan (2009) for a broader discussion of how people can coactivate work and nonwork identities when performing their job.

48. Allan Bérubé (2011a, 163) writes about barrier-crossing not only in terms of sexual identity but also in reference to social class.

49. In my case, besides the need to navigate a minority sexual identity, I also needed to handle being identified as a religious minority (the only Jewish kid in my K-12 classes) and the child of foreign parents (both my parents were born outside France). All these layers likely added to my marginality.

50. John Van Maanen reminds us that the results of fieldwork (ethnographies in particular) "display the intricate ways individuals and groups understand, accept, and resist a presumably shared order" (2011, xvii–xviii). That resistance holds true for the relationship between a fieldworker and a field as well, since other field participants treat them, at least partially, as "natives" and therefore behave with them in unique ways typical to the setting they share (Brown-Saracino 2014, 50; Katz 1982, 218).

51. The stumbling, more than the bumps per se, is what proves informative. As James Scott (1985, 310) concludes in his work on peasant resistance, the objective of a social analysis is "not somehow to tease out a consensus of agreed-upon rules and their application but rather to understand how divergent constructions of those rules and application are related to [in his case] class interests."

52. See Jane Ward (2018) for a discussion of academic gatekeepers.

53. Most fieldworkers include a brief sentence somewhere in their methods section on the relative difficulty of accessing their field but do not dwell at length on the type of pushback they encountered. As illustrations, Loïc Wacquant (2004, ix) alludes to "several months spent in a vain quest for a place where I could insert

myself to observe the local scene" before finding the gym where he would study boxers. Daniel Beunza notes in his study of Wall Street bankers that it took him "a full year, and two failed attempts, to make a successful entrée into the field" (2019, 296). And Olivier Godechot (2017, 10) explains that his examination of bonus practices in banks was "only made possible because certain interviewees . . . agreed to talk about their salaries, work, and company" but leaves us wondering about the resistance he faced when approaching all the others who refused to talk to him.

54. Some authors do spend more time on analyzing resistance. William F. Whyte's (1993) extensive appendix on the difficulties he faced when studying an Italian neighborhood in Boston is a rare, early example of such an analysis. More recently, when faced with obstacles to entering the hedge fund industry, Megan Tobias Neely (2022), for example, notes that "these obstacles yielded valuable insight into the industry's inner workings" (243). In particular, the fact that she had previously worked for a large institutional investor "actually deterred people from participating in the study" (242) and led her to better see how hedge fund managers tried not to share personal details with clients who invest in their firms. Likewise, Caitlin Zaloom (2019) writes that "the difficulties of finding students and parents who would open up about their financial situations showed me how important privacy was to middle-class families" (207), and Rachel Sherman (2019) explains that she realized ex post that her difficulty of landing interviews with self-identified "affluent" New Yorkers anticipated her "claim that many affluent people do not want to characterize themselves as such" (244). Similarly, Rene Almeling (2011) reflects on how her difficulty accessing sperm banks (as opposed to egg agencies) was "probably related to the emphasis on anonymity in sperm donation" (213). Finally, Allison Pugh (2009) remarks that it "took her years" to gain access to enough parents in one low-income school she studied, compared to other higher-income ones in her sample. She attributed that difficulty in part to the fact that lower-income parents are less socially connected than higher-income ones and participate less in school-related group activities (35–36).

55. Japonica Brown-Saracino and Muriel Darmon have perhaps most explicitly analyzed the distinct hurdles they encountered in the field and acknowledged their benefits. In her comparative study of queer communities, Brown-Saracino "came to recognize how my informants' place-specific sexual identities, and the character of local networks and institutions that emerge from and reinforce those identities, influenced their relation to the research, hindering access in a site in which women de-emphasize sexual identity, and enabling it in two others in which they celebrate their (distinct) sexual identities." (Brown-Saracino 2014, 44). She concludes that shifting "from resolving problems of access to identifying the source and significance of informants' hesitancy, and to consideration of how access relates not just to the researcher and the research but, more broadly, to informants' 'native world'" (44) is a key lesson she drew from this analysis. In Darmon's case, she tried to study psychiatric units focused on treating anorexia. One head of a unit (also a proponent of psychoanalysis) violently turned her down, while a head of a different unit (this time, more reliant on drugs for treatments) agreed. She notes that patient or operational concerns were not used to

justify the refusal. Instead, the "proper definition of the medical field and, by association, the definition and the place of sociology [vis-à-vis medicine]" motivated the refusal (Darmon 2005, 112; author's translation). Darmon warns us against strictly deducing the likelihood of refusals based on people's positioning in the psychiatric field. But she concludes that the way researchers are denied access provides an entry into medical viewpoints on anorexia and the place (or not) of a social element in this view.

Chapter One: Obstructing Access

1. Expulsions are extreme forms of obstruction, and scholars working under more authoritarian regimes—such as Gowayed (2022, 12) and Iskander (2021)—are probably at higher risk of being expelled.

2. I reached this conclusion by triangulating archival data on the acquisition and use of cadavers in New York State, forty-eight interviews with people involved in such acquisition and use, and observations for a total of fifteen days in six cadaver-procurement programs. See, for details, Anteby (2010).

3. I am not claiming that specific field dynamics "caused" the observed obstruction. Instead, I am suggesting that the obstruction was a plausible sign of these dynamics. As Michèle Lamont and Ann Swidler (2014, 166) note, only "carefully-designed multi-site ethnography can assess effects of situations" and such designs prove quite rare.

4. *Commerce* is here understood in its historical definition, namely, as the exchange between human beings of products of nature (Zelizer 2005, 293).

5. Anteby 2010.

6. Baumel 1968; Dasgupta 2004.

7. Anteby 2010, 619.

8. Goodwin 2006, 11.

9. Sappol 2002.

10. Sadler, Sadler, and Stason 1968.

11. Dalley, Driscoll, and Settles 1993, 261.

12. Gawande 2022, 27.

13. G. S. Becker and Elias 2007.

14. Anteby and Hyman 2008, 965.

15. Zerubavel 2006.

16. In other circumstances, the obstructing might signal something quite different. Consider the issue of workers' health in Amazon warehouses during the recent COVID-19 pandemic. Labor organizers concerned by this issue needed to access workers and, ideally, warehouses, so as to better understand the health risks for workers. Yet employers, like Amazon, have "the right to prohibit union organizers from setting foot on company property" and employers can even bar organizers from putting flyers on windshields in the employee parking lot (Greenhouse 2020, 113). Amazon's obstruction suggests a quite different tension present in the field: the company's fear of unionization.

17. Bechky 2021, 192.

18. Ibid, 75.

19. Timmermans 2007, 30.

20. The snowballing sampling strategy is often highly effective when research-ing stigmatized topics or populations. Once a legitimate insider can vouch for the interloper, others are more likely to trust them. See for another example Alya Guseva's (2020, 162) discussion of accessing the Russian banking system.

21. Sudhir Venkatesh's study into sex work in New York City in 1997 illus-trates well such a movement online of distributed activities. Each time he tried delving deeper into a neighborhood historically associated with prostitution (e.g., Times Squares, Lower East Side) to conduct fieldwork, local residents would tell him "everyone moved" (Venkatesh 2013, 691). Since then, of course, countless other activities, legal or not, have moved online.

22. Expressing outrage for being "studied" is a classic move used to confront interlopers, and one that requires further probing. As an example, Terry Williams (1996) reports similar outrage in his study of cocaine users. At a gay night in a New York City club, a patron suddenly turned to his companion and shouted in a loud voice for everyone (including the researcher) to hear: "He [Williams] wants to do research on us. You scum bag! What do we look like, pal? Fucking guinea pigs? You've got some nerve walking in here, talking about doing research!" (30). Williams later learned that the man was an off-duty police officer—someone who perhaps had the most to lose if outed as gay or as a drug user in his workplace.

23. Anteby 2013b.

Chapter Two: Hiding from View

1. All names (including the airport's and the student's) are pseudonyms to protect anonymity.

2. This finding around visibility/invisibility dynamics emerged from a com-prehensive analysis of eighty-nine interviewees with TSA respondents (Anteby and Chan 2018).

3. The student gave me permission to reproduce her email.

4. See Glaeser (2000) and Van Maanen (1973) for examples of police officers trusting only their own.

5. de Rond 2017, 134.

6. Ibid, 135.

7. The Ministry of Defense's attempts to hide the troubling issue of civilian casualties included pressuring the vice chancellor of the book author's university to intervene, delaying replies to the author for months, and providing long, detailed lists of objections to specific written points.

8. Solans 2013, 98.

9. USGA 2013, 20.

10. USGA 2012, 13.

11. Kosatka 2011, 34.

12. Ayn Cavicchi, Curtis Chan, and I conducted interviews with TSA employ-ees in 2011 and 2012.

13. This example builds on the study I conducted with Curtis Chan on surveillance and invisibility at the Transportation Security Administration. I thank him for being such an engaged collaborator.

14. Approximately 5 percent of TSA's workforce received a reprimand or a higher sanction at the airport we studied that year, and this disciplinary process could result in restrictions preventing screeners from applying for promotions or receiving bonuses.

15. See Janet Vertesi (2015) for an example of a fieldworker reporting methodological limitation due to her citizenship. As she explains when interacting with National Aeronautics and Space Administration staff members, "Not being a United States citizen, I was limited to discussing and witnessing the scientific side of the [Mars] mission, avoiding any discussion of technical details of the rovers and their operations and all situations when the latter details would be discussed or displayed" (19).

16. Jennifer Croissant (2014) identifies "intentionality" as a key dimension of the production of "non-knowledge" (6). Here, I do not consider intentionality to be a necessary condition for defense mechanisms to flourish.

17. Gide, 21.
18. Ibid, 25.
19. Taussig 2010, 167.
20. Blee 2008, 2.
21. Ibid, 50.
22. Adler 2017, 144.
23. Jerolmack and Murphy 2019.
24. Aziz 2009, 41.
25. Pascoe 2007, 181.
26. Ibid, 190.
27. Ibid, 181.

Chapter Three: Shelving

1. For another example of the Harvard Business School's alleged concerns about its brand, see *Benjamin Edelman vs. President and Fellows of Harvard College*, 2023, Suffolk Superior Court, Commonwealth of Massachusetts. This complaint by a former HBS faculty member against the school alleges that "repeatedly, HBS made decisions motivated by public relations, political concerns, and personal animus" when conducting a "faculty review board" of his case to determine whether he had engaged in any misconduct (2).

2. This shaming is a typical behavior at Harvard Business School that John Van Maanen already noted decades ago (Van Maanen 1983).

3. The committee on culture did ultimately come up with recommendations, some of which I suspect got implemented. Yet I still got the sense that more people than not (outside the committee) wanted the school to remain as it was rather than see it truly evolve.

4. (Bowen 1964). In David Riesman's preface to her book, he notes that he was told by Laura Bohannan's friends that she used a pen name "to protect the tribe" but adds, "the thought crossed my mind that the author herself may have feared that the book might hurt her reputation as a competent and objective ethnographer" (xvi).

5. The Disney California Adventure (DCA) Park is a theme park located at the Disneyland Resort in Anaheim, California. For simplicity reasons, I will refer to the DCA Park in the rest of the text as the Disneyland Resort.

6. Eades 2017.

7. See D. Miller (2017). The NLRB determined that three workers had been illegally fired for their union activities, and the Walt Disney Corporation was ordered to pay each of them $3,000.

8. See *Settlement in the Matter of Walt Disney Parks and Resorts U.S., Inc.* 2015. Cases 21-CA-156727 and 160252. National Labor Relations Board.

9. D. Miller 2017.

10. These quotes come from a set of interviews that Bella T. Fong and I conducted with Disney puppeteers.

11. Shelving is a form of "surface bargaining" or what Shieber (1973) defines as "employer bargaining that is not 'a bona fide effort to arrive at a collective bargaining agreement'" (658).

12. Van Maanen 1991.

13. This control is evident by puppeteers sometimes listing themselves on official documents by another profession, in part to improve their status in the eyes of the authorities when seeking permits to perform (McCormick 2013).

14. See *Alhovsky v. New York City Dep't of Parks & Rec.*, 2014, U.S. Dist. LEXIS 115913, United States District Court for the Southern District of New York.

15. See City of Hickory, NC, 2020, Code of Ordinances, Sec. 24–15.

16. See *Christ v. Town of Ocean City*, 2018, 312 F. Supp. 3d 465, United States District Court for the District of Maryland.

17. *Hobbs v. County of Westchester.* 2005. 397 F.3d 133, United States Court of Appeals for the Second Circuit.

18. Bell 2008, 97–98.

19. See *State of New York*, 2016, *NY S.B. 7944. 239th Annual Legislative Session*; and *AFL-CIO v. City of Miami*, 2011, 637 F.3d 1178, United States Court of Appeals for the Eleventh Circuit.

20. The Jim Henson Company has historically treated its puppeteers (even when performing in nonunion jobs) better than other employers. The fact that the company's founder was a puppeteer himself explains in part this anomaly.

21. *Sid & Marty Krofft TV Prods. v. McDonald's Corp*, 1977, 562 F.2d 1157, United States Court of Appeals for the Ninth Circuit. Note that an earlier US court ruling on the issue of a puppets' ownership focused on the puppet's material construction (and whether it could be patented), but not a puppet's character (*Cohen v. Bunin*, 1944, 183 Misc. 90, Supreme Court of New York, Special Term, New York County).

22. *Jim Henson Prods. v. John T. Brady & Assocs*, 1997, 16 F. Supp. 2d 259, United States District Court for the Southern District of New York.

23. The same court did consider the possibility of decoupling puppets from puppeteers, since the Screen Actors Guild code distinguished in the 1950s between situations in which advertisers owned the puppet and situations in which the puppeteer owned the puppet.

24. *Jim Henson Prods. v. John T. Brady & Assocs*, 1997, 16 F. Supp. 2d 259, United States District Court for the Southern District of New York.

25. By screen work, I mean work for puppeteers on movie, television, and streaming sets.

26. *Detroit Inst. of Arts Founders Soc'y v. Rose*, 2001, 127 F. Supp. 2d 117, United States District Court for the District of Connecticut.

27. Andrews and Schmidt 2017.

28. Deb and Haigney 2017.

29. Parker 2017.

30. Bitette 2017.

31. When they decided to unionize, the puppeteers' pay ranged from $12.59 to $17 per hour depending on their seniority (though the top earner made $23.07 per hour) (D. Miller 2017).

32. The puppeteers' circumstances at Disneyland were not unique at the park: nearly 75 percent of Disneyland employees were unable to afford "basic living expenses" without a second job (Dreier and Flaming 2020). For more context on the labor conditions at Disneyland, see the critical documentary codirected by the granddaughter of the Walt Disney Company cofounder Roy Disney and titled *The American Dream and Other Fairy Tales* (Disney and Hughes 2022).

33. Others have reported contentious relationships and attempted sabotage of contract negotiations between labor unions and the Disney parks in California and Florida (see, for example, Pedicini 2016; Rozsa 2017).

34. Stark 2020, 609.

35. Clokie and Robinson 1937, 125–26.

36. Davis 2016.

37. Pfeffer and Salancik 1978.

38. D. Miller 2017.

39. Clokie and Robinson 1937.

40. Butcher and Pronckutė 2019, 84.

41. Boston University is not immune to such shelving.

Chapter Four: Silencing

1. I would be remiss not to mention that this setup of a "case protagonist" sitting at her desk, looking out a window, and facing a seemingly high-stakes decision is the classic start of many HBS cases.

2. The name is a pseudonym. I am grateful to this person for having shared this anecdote with me shortly after reading my book presenting the results of my study of Harvard Business School faculty socialization.

3. Galeota 1969.

4. The only time the school suspended regular instructions for an extended period of time was from 1943 to 1945, during the Second World War.

5. Jennifer Croissant (2014) explains well the distinction between a silence that suggests that "things go without saying" versus one that hints to "things unspeakable and forbidden" (15). In the HBS context, the silence was more within the realm of the unspeakable.

6. Anteby 2013a.

7. Homans 1993, 468.

8. Winter 2010, 3.

9. Abend 2014; Khurana 2007; Schleef 2005.

10. Cruikshank 1987, 44.

11. George F. Baker cited by Wallace B. Donham (1925, 122).

12. Kunda 2009.

13. Sweeney 2008.

14. Broughton 2009.

15. Abend 2014, 48.

16. Orta 2019, 165.

17. Boltanski and Chiapello 1999; Both 2007.

18. See Anteby (2016) for more details on the contents of HBS teaching notes.

19. Anteby 2016.

20. Gragg 1940, 35.

21. Bugental 1978.

22. Ibid, 178.

23. See Anteby (2013a) for a longer discussion of other instances of silence at the school.

24. 1996, 199; see also Vaughan 2002.

25. Missteps are wonderful ways to learn about shared expectations. While naively trying to take field notes during a stand-up comedy show, Patrick Reilly (2018) was immediate reprimanded by the club's staff. That person "jetted over to my direction and loudly hurled a stern directive at me: 'No writing in the room!' . . . people see someone writing, they get afraid about stealing jokes" (939). Joke-stealing gradually became the focus of Reilly's inquiry.

26. Karabel 2005.

27. My claim is not that this silencing was intentional at HBS. Like for Rene Almeling (2020), the broad domain of knowledge that was missing in my context and in hers was "not caused by *intentional* obfuscation" (169, my emphasis). Instead, she describes the missing science of men's reproductive health as the result of the interplay between dynamics that rendered certain questions "unthinkable" (169).

28. This reader only raised minor points around publicizing HBS's average pay figure. The data came however from Harvard University's provost's public website.

29. This reader did leave open the possibility that I had reported my project to the dean via another planning process in place at the school, by noting, "Perhaps he [Michel] described this project in the 'Big Ideas' section of the

planning form [required by the school] . . . seen only by the Dean." I don't recall doing so.

30. I cannot remember for how many years I mentioned this project in my annual reporting before deciding to stop doing so, since I did not keep traces of all my reports. I do know I included it at least in my 2008 and 2009 reports, and everyone in my department as well as the dean knew about my desire to pursue it.

31. Petriglieri, Ashford, and Wrzesniewski 2019.

32. Zerubavel 2010, 33.

33. Ibid, 37.

34. As Georg Simmel (1906) explains, "the secret of the one party is to a certain extent recognized by the other, and the intentionally or unintentionally concealed is intentionally or unintentionally respected" (462). Members' uniformity helps immensely for such recognition to occur.

35. Keenan 2013, xxiv.

36. Keenan 2013, 51; Goffman 1961.

37. Anteby 2013a, 112.

38. I thank this faculty member for allowing me to reproduce part of the letter sent to the university president.

39. Almeling 2020, 128.

40. Verdery 2018, 297.

Chapter Five: Forgetting

1. Luker 2008, 149.

2. Rabinow 1977, 31.

3. See Bayurgil (2022, 1097), Guseva (2020, 162–63), Verdery (2018).

4. I thank Daniel Beunza, my fellow NYU doctoral student at the time, for teaching me this basic field trick: saying even before you set foot in a field that you *are* studying a topic rather than that you *want* to study it.

5. My research affiliation at the time, the Paris Institute of Political Science, is commonly referred to as "Sciences Po" in France.

6. Luckily, I never shared with anyone at the plant that my maternal grandparents had been born in Germany. Even though they fled Nazi Germany in 1938, the double German and American ties might have made it even harder for me to "access" the site. At the same time, the precise fact that I had these connections and needed to deftly navigate them made me the perfect match for this site.

7. Bodemer and Laugier 1996.

8. Many other examples of France trying to promote a national leader in a given industry permeate French history. For details of such attempts in the nuclear and biotech industries, see respectively Hecht (1998) and Rabinow (2002).

9. The research I conducted with Virág Molnár on the topic of forgetting in organizations heavily informs this chapter (Anteby and Molnar 2012). I am very grateful to her for this fruitful collaboration and for helping me navigate the literature on memory.

10. Hecht 1998, 2.

11. Audrieu 1987, 252.

12. SNECMA annual report, 1956, 18–19.

13. Bodemer 1986, 117.

14. Bohnekamp 2002; Lamouche 1999.

15. Carlier 1997.

16. Hunt 1991.

17. Anteby and Molnar 2012, 526.

18. Chilin 2000, 84.

19. Retirement gifts were only the tip of the iceberg of artifacts produced illegally on company time and with company materials. Window frames, cutlery, barbecues, and other artifacts were more common than the prized and elaborate retirement gifts that I initially focused on.

20. SNECMA annual report, 2004, 34.

21. Harris, Campbell, and Brophy 2019.

22. Scranton 2013, 124.

23. Nouzille 1999.

24. Anteby and Molnar 2012, 526.

25. Elias 2006.

26. Fayard and Weeks 2007.

27. When studying affluent New Yorkers, Rachel Sherman (2019) reports also being self-conscious about the car she drove. As she recalls, "The first time I planned to drive out to the suburbs to conduct an interview, I felt anxious about my 1994 Honda Civic. It had giant white patches on the roof and hood, products of years of East Coast winter street parking, which stood out against the dark blue of the rest of the car. I was afraid the state of the car might make my interviewees see me as impoverished and thus not talk openly with me" (248–49).

28. Annette Lareau's (2021) guide to conducting interviews and participant observations contains many insights on how to dress in the field. When discussing the clothing worn by field researchers, she notes, "How the participants perceive you makes a difference in the level of trust that they extend to you." (49).

29. Even the group's nickname, "O," was a way to forget it's German origin. Referring to its full name (Oestrich) would have evoked the group's German origins.

30. Anteby and Molnar 2012.

31. Wacquant 2004, 264.

32. Van Maanen and Kolb 1985, 24.

33. Scheper-Hughes 2001, xiii.

34. Connerton 2008.

35. Olick and Robbins 1998, 117.

Chapter Six: Denying

1. All conversations with this ghostwriter were in French. I therefore translated the exchanges. There are two terms in French for a ghostwriter: a historical term ("nègre") and a more accepted, contemporary one ("prête-plume"). The ghostwriter used neither of them when describing his work.

2. Many of the findings in this chapter come from my collaboration with Nicholas Occhiuto on ghostwriters of memoirs. I thank him for his many insights and for endlessly filling my huge gaps in knowledge on US celebrities and sports culture.

3. The findings reported in this chapter result from an analysis of seventy-two interviews with ghostwriters and publishing industry insiders. For details on the data, sampling, and analytical methods see Anteby and Occhiuto 2020.

4. All names in this chapter are pseudonyms.

5. Zerubavel 2006, 47.

6. Cohen 2001, 3.

7. Lindhout and Corbett 2013.

8. Trump 1987.

9. Many of the ghostwriters we ended up interviewing were subsequently identified in the acknowledgment sections of *NYT* bestselling memoirs.

10. Agassi 2009: 387.

11. Erdal 2009, xii.

12. Coser, Kadushin, and Powell 1982; Dody 1980; James-Enger 2013; McDonald 2003; Moffatt and Elliott 2007; Moskin 2012; Murphey 2017; Ross et al. 2008.

13. Crofts 2004; James-Enger 2013; Joy 2014; S. Miller and Santana 2017; Murphey 2017; Shaw 2003; 2012; Whitworth 2015.

14. Shaw 2003, 16.

15. Crofts 2004.

16. Barley and Kunda 2004; Bidwell et al. 2013; Kalleberg 2011; Weil 2014.

17. Anteby and Occhiuto 2020.

18. Mazza 2017.

19. Zerubavel 2006, 47.

20. Cohen 2001, x.

21. Cohen 2001, 7–9.

22. Gillard et al. 2021, 9, author's translation.

23. Kahn 2015, 127.

Conclusion

1. H. S. Becker 1971, 15.

2. Many scholars have underlined the key role of abduction in analyzing field data; the doubts and surprises that field defenses often generate for interlopers can be critical to the shaping of a research inquiry. See Locke, Golden-Biddle, and Feldman (2008) and Timmermans and Tavory (2012, 2022).

3. As Howard Becker notes, "We need to investigate those cases in which access has been achieved easily and those where it proved difficult or impossible" (H. S. Becker 1971, 17).

4. Lareau 2021, 262.

5. This invitation to grapple more fully with hurdles echoes recent calls to investigate "more fully the structures and processes that impede the production of knowledge" (Kempner, Merz, and Bosk 2011, 475).

6. Rabinow 1977, 154.

7. Croissant 2014, 7.

8. Social movements, open communities, and transformational organizations offer examples of fields that often can rapidly embrace scholars trying to access them. Kathleen Blee (2008) was surprised by how rapidly former women members of the Ku Klux Klan welcomed her (a white female). Their welcome echoed the one they had traditionally extended to all white Protestant women who lived around them when the Klan thrived. Siobhán O'Mahony and Fabrizio Ferraro (2007), who study open-source software communities, seemed welcomed by participants who prided themselves in operating openly. And Patrick Sheehan notes that "in all three [job] clubs [studied], I introduced myself and my research project to club leaders on my first day of attendance and was warmly welcomed" (2021, 478). Club leaders were keen to help clients transform themselves, so helping a doctoral candidate earn his degree translated as just another instance of helping someone transform.

9. Van Maanen 2020.

10. What might code as a form of methodological "queer persistence" (Stone 2018) is intimately linked, at least for me, to a form of queer liberation when success ensues.

11. Katz 1988.

12. Carlsen and Dutton 2011.

13. Beckman and Mazmanian 2020, 185.

14. Sallaz 2009, 254–55.

15. Maitlis 2011, 76; Vaughan 2021, 9.

16. For an exception, see Amy L. Stone's (2018) report of a moment of experiencing a field "high" when they landed upon a coveted document while mining an archive with students. As they "yell" and start opening the folder, they feel "chills running up and down" their arms (216–17).

17. As Devah Pager once reminded one of her doctoral students, one "should not avoid collecting certain data just because it might be difficult" (cited by Clair 2020, 200).

18. Joanna Kempner and her coauthors (2011) point out that "knowledge production is biased toward the benefit of the privileged, leaving blank spaces where knowledge could empower disenfranchised social groups" (478).

Coda

1. Meadow 2013.

2. Wacquant 2005.

3. Japonica Brown-Saracino (2014, 66) notes that scholars facing "blocked access" should ask themselves, among other questions, "Is it them [i.e., field participants]?" but also "Is it me?"

4. Senior was referring to Brickman's quest as well as her own writing on him, since depression also ran in her family (Senior 2020).

5. Wacquant 2004, xi.

6. The idea of dancing in the field echoes Kristin Luker's and Ashley Rubin's use of vivid metaphors, respectively salsa dancing and rock climbing, to capture research pursuits' sensations (Luker 2008; Rubin 2021).

7. Mary Ann Glynn (2011) writes, for instance, about the interplay between her object of study (i.e., the entrepreneur Martha Stewart) and her own interests. She sees resonance between the idea of creating a "Martha moment," or a glimpse (good or bad) into one's life and the larger sphere of living one has fostered in others, and her own pursuits.

8. The idea that queer scholars bring unique skill sets to their work has recently been put forward (Compton, Meadow, and Schilt 2018). More broadly, however, generations of queer individuals (not only scholars) who dealt with significant social backlash likely developed unique ways to handle their social surroundings (Canaday 2023). Such a socialization might even have led them to specialize in certain jobs calling for such abilities (Bérubé 2011b; Tilcsik, Anteby, and Knight 2015).

9. Van Maanen 2011, 2.

10. Agar 1996, 4.

11. A bit later, when one of my professors in graduate school in the United States addressed our class by starting a sentence with "when you get married . . . ," I was quick to pen a letter to the student newspaper reminding faculty and readers that *not* all of us could yet legally marry. We were at the height of the US government's "don't ask, don't tell" policy, and denials were everywhere, not only in my family's realm.

12. I do not wish to underplay the likely real fears that my coming out triggered for my parents and others. They later admitted fearing that I was HIV-positive, since I came of age in the midst of the AIDS crisis and prior to the advent of life-saving triple therapies. For details on how defenses ease anxiety see Freud (1966).

13. Stone 2018.

14. It is obviously easier for someone to write ex post (rather than ex ante) about what might have informed their research pursuits. By positioning this coda at the end of the book, my intent is to acknowledge this limitation. The reimagined view of self should not provide a false sense of explanation or be seen as a magical master key to one's trajectory. The "self" I describe is as much the result of my pursuits as their impetus.

Abend, Gabriel. 2014. *The Moral Background: An Inquiry into the History of Business Ethics*. Princeton, NJ: Princeton University Press.

Adler, Hans Günther. 2017. *Theresienstadt 1941–1945: The Face of a Coerced Community*. New York: Cambridge University Press.

Agar, Michael. 1996. *The Professional Stranger: An Informal Introduction to Ethnography*. 2nd ed. San Diego, CA: Academic Press.

Agassi, Andre. 2009. *Open: An Autobiography*. New York: Knopf.

Almeling, Rene. 2011. *Sex Cells: The Medical Market for Eggs and Sperm*. Berkeley, CA: University of California Press.

———. 2020. *Guynecology: The Missing Science of Men's Reproductive Health*. Oakland, CA: University of California Press.

Alvesson, Mats, and Kaj Sköldberg. 2018. *Reflexive Methodology: New Vistas for Qualitative Research*. Thousand Oaks, CA: Sage.

Anderson, Elijah. 1989. *A Place on the Corner*. Chicago, IL: University of Chicago Press.

Andrews, Travis M., and Samantha Schmidt. 2017. "Muppet Creator's Family Says Fired Actor Played Kermit as 'Bitter, Angry, Depressed Victim.'" *Washington Post*, July 19, 2017, sec. Morning Mix. https://www.washingtonpost.com/news/morning-mix/wp/2017/07/19/muppet-creators-family-says-fired-actor-played-kermit-as-bitter-depressed-victim/.

Anteby, Michel. 2010. "Markets, Morals, and Practices of Trade: Jurisdictional Disputes in the U.S. Commerce in Cadavers." *Administrative Science Quarterly*, 55 (4): 606–38.

———. 2013a. *Manufacturing Morals: The Values of Silence in Business School Education*. Chicago, IL: University of Chicago Press.

———. 2013b. "Relaxing the Taboo on Telling Our Own Stories: Upholding Professional Distance and Personal Involvement." *Organization Science* 24 (4): 1277–90.

———. 2016. "The Ideology of Silence at the Harvard Business School: Structuring Faculty's Teaching Tasks for Moral Relativism." *Research in the Sociology of Organizations: The Structuring of Work in Organizations*, no. 47, 103–21.

Anteby, Michel, and Curtis K. Chan. 2018. "A Self-Fulfilling Cycle of Coercive Surveillance: Workers' Invisibility Practices and Managerial Justification." *Organization Science* 29 (2): 247–63.

Anteby, Michel, and Mikell Hyman. 2008. "Entrepreneurial Ventures and Whole-Body Donations: A Regional Perspective from the United States." *Social Science & Medicine* 66 (4): 963–69.

Anteby, Michel, and Virag Molnar. 2012. "Collective Memory Meets Organizational Identity: Remembering to Forget in a Firm's Rhetorical History." *Academy of Management Journal* 55 (3): 515–40.

Anteby, Michel, and Nicholas Occhiuto. 2020. "Stand-in Labor and the Rising Economy of Self." *Social Forces* 98 (3): 1287–310.

Anthony, Callen. 2021. "When Knowledge Work and Analytical Technologies Collide: The Practices and Consequences of Black Boxing Algorithmic Technologies." *Administrative Science Quarterly* 66 (4): 1173–212.

Audrieu, C. 1987. "Des Nationalisations Disparates." In *Les Nationalisations de La Libération*, edited by C. Audrieu, L. Le Van, and A. Prost, 250–66. Paris: Presses de la Foundation Nationale des Sciences Politiques.

Aziz, Sahar F. 2009. "Sticks and Stones, the Words That Hurt: Entrenched Stereotypes Eight Years after 9/11." *New York City Law Review* 13 (1): 33–72.

Banaszak, Lee Ann. 1996. *Why Movements Succeed or Fail: Opportunity, Culture, and the Struggle for Woman Suffrage.* Princeton, NJ: Princeton University Press.

Barley, Stephen R. 2004. "Puddle Jumping as a Career Strategy." In *Renewing Research Practice: Lessons from Scholar's Journeys*, edited by Ralph E. Stablein and Peter J. Frost, 67–82. Stanford, CA: Stanford University Press.

Barley, Stephen R., and Gideon Kunda. 2004. *Gurus, Hired Guns, and Warm Bodies: Itinerant Experts in a Knowledge Economy.* Princeton, NJ: Princeton University Press.

Baumel, J. J. 1968. "Donation of Bodies for Medical Education." *The Nebraska State Medical Journal* 53 (3): 90.

Bayurgil, Ladin. 2022. "Fired and Evicted: Istanbul Doorkeepers' Strategies of Navigating Employment and Housing Precarity." *Social Problems* 69 (4): 1092–108.

Bechky, Beth A. 2021. *Blood, Powder, and Residue: How Crime Labs Translate Evidence into Proof.* Princeton, NJ: Princeton University Press.

Becker, Gary S., and Julio Jorge Elias. 2007. "Introducing Incentives in the Market for Live and Cadaveric Organ Donations." *Journal of Economic Perspectives* 21 (3): 3–24.

Becker, Howard S. 1971. *Sociological Work.* New Brunswick, NJ: Transaction Publishers.

Becker, Howard S., and Blanche Geer. 1957. "Participant Observation and Interviewing: A Comparison." *Human Organization* 16 (3): 28–32.

Beckert, Jens, and Matías Dewey, eds. 2017. *The Architecture of Illegal Markets: Towards an Economic Sociology of Illegality in the Economy.* Oxford: Oxford University Press.

Beckman, Christine M., and Melissa Mazmanian. 2020. *Dreams of the Overworked: Living, Working, and Parenting in the Digital Age.* Stanford, CA: Stanford University Press.

Bell, John. 2008. *American Puppet Modernism.* New York: Palgrave Macmillan.

Bernstein, Ethan S. 2012. "The Transparency Paradox: A Role for Privacy in Organizational Learning and Operational Control." *Administrative Science Quarterly* 57 (2): 181–216.

Bérubé, Allan. 2011a. *My Desire for History: Essays in Gay, Community, and Labor History*. Chapel Hill: University of North Carolina Press.

———. 2011b. "'Queer Work' and Labor History." In *My Desire for History: Essays in Gay, Community, and Labor History*, 259–69. Chapel Hill: University of North Carolina Press.

Beunza, Daniel. 2019. *Taking the Floor: Models, Morals, and Management in a Wall Street Trading Room*. Princeton, NJ: Princeton University Press.

Bidwell, Matthew, Forrest Briscoe, Isabel Fernandez-Mateo, and Adina Sterling. 2013. "The Employment Relationship and Inequality: How and Why Changes in Employment Practices Are Reshaping Rewards in Organizations." *The Academy of Management Annals* 7 (1): 61–121.

Bitette, Nicole. 2017. "Kermit the Frog Actor Denies He Was Difficult to Work With." *New York Daily News*, July 20, 2017. http://www.nydailynews.com /entertainment/gossip/kermit-frog-actor-denies-difficult-work-article-1 .3341288.

Blee, Kathleen M. 2008. *Women of the Klan: Racism and Gender in the 1920s*. Berkeley, CA: University of California Press.

Bodemer, Alfred. 1986. "De l'Hélice à l'Aviation à Réaction (Moteurs Militaires)." Colloque de l'Aéronautique à l'Espace, Paris.

Bodemer, Alfred, and Robert Laugier. 1996. *L'ATAR et Tous les Autres Moteurs à Réaction Français*. Riquewihr, France: Editions J.D. Reber.

Bohnekamp, Dorothea. 2002. "Les Ingénieurs Allemands dans l'Industrie Française d'Armement entre 1945 et 1950." *Revue d'Allemagne* 34 (1): 29–44.

Boltanski, Luc, and Eve Chiapello. 1999. *Le Nouvel Esprit du Capitalisme*. Paris: Gallimard.

Both, Anne. 2007. *Les Managers et Leurs Discours: Anthropologie de La Rhétorique Managériale*. Bordeaux, France: Presses Universitaire de Bordeaux.

Bourdieu, Pierre, and Loïc Wacquant. 1992. *An Invitation to Reflexive Sociology*. Chicago, IL: University of Chicago Press.

Bowen, Elenore Smith. 1964. *Return to Laughter: An Anthropological Novel*. New York: Anchor.

Brim, Matt, and Amin Ghaziani. 2016. "Introduction: Queer Methods." *Women's Studies Quarterly* 44 (3/4): 14–27.

Broughton, Philip Delves. 2009. *What They Teach You at Harvard Business School: My Two Years inside the Cauldron of Capitalism*. London: Penguin Books.

Brown-Saracino, Japonica. 2014. "From Methodological Stumbles to Substantive Insights: Gaining Ethnographic Access in Queer Communities." *Qualitative Sociology* 37 (1): 43–68.

Bugental, James F. T. 1978. "The Silence of the Sky." In *Interpersonal Behavior: Communication and Understanding in Relationships*, edited by A. G. Athos and J. J. Gabarro, 176–85. Englewood Cliffs, NJ: Prentice-Hall.

Butcher, Paul, and Simona Pronckutė. 2019. "European Citizens' Consultations: Consultation Begins at Home." *European View* 18 (1): 80–88.

Canaday, Margot. 2023. *Queer Career: Sexuality and Work in Modern America.* Princeton, NJ: Princeton University Press.

Carlier, Claude. 1997. "Le 'Groupe O' (1945–1960)." Presented at the Institut Historique Allemand, Paris. http://www.stratisc.org/ihcc_GROUPO.html.

Carlsen, Arne, and Jane E. Dutton. 2011. *Research Alive: Exploring Generative Moments in Doing Qualitative Research.* Liber: Copenhagen Business School Press.

Childress, Clayton. 2017. *Under the Cover: The Creation, Production, and Reception of a Novel.* Princeton, NJ: Princeton University Press.

Chilin, R. 2000. "Une Section Syndicale Face à la Réalité." In *Pages d'Histoire Syndicale: La CFTC-CFDT SNECMA-Villaroche, 1947–1980,* edited by Roger Mullié and R. Chilin, 17–102. Paris: Editions L'Harmattan.

Clair, Matthew. 2020. *Privilege and Punishment: How Race and Class Matter in Criminal Court.* Princeton, NJ: Princeton University Press.

Clokie, Hugh McDowall, and Joseph William Robinson. 1937. *Royal Commissions of Inquiry: The Significance of Investigations in British Politics.* Stanford, CA: Stanford University Press.

Cohen, Stanley. 2001. *States of Denial: Knowing about Atrocities and Suffering.* Cambridge, UK: Polity Press.

Compton, D'Lane R., Tey Meadow, and Kristen Schilt, eds. 2018. *Other, Please Specify: Queer Methods in Sociology.* Oakland, CA: University of California Press.

Connerton, Paul. 2008. "Seven Types of Forgetting." *Memory Studies* 1 (1): 59–71.

Coser, Lewis A., Charles Kadushin, and Walter W Powell. 1982. *Books: The Culture and Commerce of Publishing.* New York: Basic Books.

Cousin, Bruno, Shamus Khan, and Ashley Mears. 2018. "Theoretical and Methodological Pathways for Research on Elites." *Socio-Economic Review* 16 (2): 225–49.

Crofts, Andrew. 2004. *Ghostwriting.* Boston, MA: A&C Black.

Croissant, Jennifer L. 2014. "Agnotology: Ignorance and Absence; or, Towards a Sociology of Things That Aren't There." *Social Epistemology* 28 (1): 4–25.

Cruikshank, Jeffrey L. 1987. *A Delicate Experiment: The Harvard Business School, 1908–1945.* Boston, MA: Harvard Business Press.

Dalley, Arthur F., Robert E. Driscoll, and Harry E. Settles. 1993. "The Uniform Anatomical Gift Act: What Every Clinical Anatomist Should Know." *Clinical Anatomy* 6 (4): 247–54.

Darmon, Muriel. 2005. "Le Psychiatre, la Sociologue et la Boulangère: Analyse d'un Refus de Terrain." *Genèses,* no. 1, 98–112.

Dasgupta, Neela. 2004. "Unclaimed Bodies at the Anatomy Table." *Journal of the American Medical Association* 291 (1): 122–23.

Davis, Gerald F. 2016. *The Vanishing American Corporation: Navigating the Hazards of a New Economy.* Oakland, CA: Berrett-Koehler Publishers.

Deb, Sopan, and Sophie Haigney. 2017. "Kermit the Frog Performer and Disney Spar Over an Ugly 'Muppet' Firing." *The New York Times*, July 18, 2017, sec. Arts B.5.

De Rond, Mark. 2017. *Doctors at War: Life and Death in a Field Hospital*. Ithaca, NY: Cornell University Press.

Desmond, Matthew. 2007. *On the Fireline: Living and Dying with Wildland Firefighters*. Chicago, IL: University of Chicago Press.

Disney, Abigail, and Kathleen Hughes, dirs. 2022. *The American Dream and Other Fairy Tales*. Chicago Media Project & Fork Films.

Dody, Sandford. 1980. *Giving Up the Ghost: A Writer's Life among the Stars*. New York: M. Evans.

Donham, W. B. 1925. "Report of the President and Treasurer of Harvard College 1923–1924." Cambridge, MA: Official Register of Harvard University.

Dreier, Peter, and Daniel Flaming. 2020. "Working for the Mouse: A Survey of Disneyland Resort Employees." *Context* 19 (1): 24–29.

Eades, Mark. 2017. "Disney Junior Show Ending at California Adventure as Puppeteers Negotiate Pay Raise." *Orange County Register*, February 17, 2017. https://www.ocregister.com/articles/disney-744284-live-puppeteers.html.

Elias, Norbert. 2006. *The Court Society*. Dublin: University College Dublin Press.

Erdal, Jennie. 2009. *Ghosting: A Double Life*. New York: Anchor.

Evans, Joelle, Ruthanne Huising, and Susan S. Silbey. 2015. "Accounting for Accounts: Crafting Ethnographic Validity through Team Ethnography." In *Handbook of Qualitative Organizational Research*, edited by Kimberly D. Elsbach and Roderick M. Kramer, 143–55. New York: Routledge.

Fayard, Anne-Laure, and John Weeks. 2007. "Photocopiers and Water-Coolers: The Affordances of Informal Interaction." *Organization Studies* 28 (5): 605–34.

Feldman, Martha S., Jeannine Bell, and Michele Tracy Berger. 2004. *Gaining Access: A Practical and Theoretical Guide for Qualitative Researchers*. Walnut Creek, CA: Rowman Altamira.

Fine, Gary Alan. 2007. *Authors of the Storm: Meteorologists and the Culture of Prediction*. Chicago, IL: University of Chicago Press.

Freud, Anna. 1966. *The Ego and the Mechanisms of Defense*. New York: International Universities Press.

Galeota, William R. 1969. "Class Attendance Falls Drastically as Harvard Observes Moratorium." *Harvard Crimson*, October 16, 1969.

Gawande, Atul. 2002. *Complications: Notes from the Life of a Young Surgeon*. New York: Penguin Books.

Gerson, Kathleen, and Sarah Damaske. 2020. *The Science and Art of Interviewing*. Oxford: Oxford University Press.

Gibson-Light, Michael, and Josh Seim. 2020. "Punishing Fieldwork: Penal Domination and Prison Ethnography." *Journal of Contemporary Ethnography* 49 (5): 666–90.

Gide, André. 1937. *Return from the U.S.S.R.* Translated by Dorothy Bussy. New York: Alfred A. Knopf.

Gillard, Cristelle, Patrick Lavaure, Olivier Sidokpohou, and Sophie Bergerat. 2021. "Mission d'Inspection à Sciences Po Paris suite à la Démission du Président de la Fondation Nationale des Sciences Politiques." nos. 2021-28. Paris: Inspection Générale de l'Education, du Sport et de la Recherche.

Glaeser, Andreas. 2000. *Divided in Unity: Identity, Germany, and the Berlin Police*. Chicago, IL: University of Chicago Press.

Glynn, Mary Ann. 2011. "The 'Martha' Moment: Wading into Others' Worlds." In *Research Alive: Generative Moments for Doing Qualitative Research*, edited by Arne Carlsen and Jane E. Dutton, Copenhagen Business School Press, 63–66. Liber, Sweden: Copenhagen Business School Press Copenhagen.

Godart, Frédéric, Greta Hsu, and Giacomo Negro. 2023. "Gatekeeping and the Use of Contested Practices in Creative Industries: The Case of Fur in Fashion." *Organization Science* 34 (2): 637–56.

Godart, Frédéric, and Ashley Mears. 2009. "How Do Cultural Producers Make Creative Decisions? Lessons from the Catwalk." *Social Forces* 88 (2): 671–92.

Godechot, Olivier. 2017. *Wages, Bonuses and Appropriation of Profit in the Financial Industry: The Working Rich*. New York: Routledge.

Goffman, Erving. 1961. *Asylums: Essays on the Social Situation of Mental Patients and Other Inmates*. Garden City, NY: Anchor Books.

———. 1989. "On Fieldwork." *Journal of Contemporary Ethnography* 18 (2): 123–32.

Goodwin, Michele. 2006. *Black Markets: The Supply and Demand of Body Parts*. Cambridge: Cambridge University Press.

Gowayed, Heba. 2022. *Refuge: How the State Shapes Human Potential*. Princeton, NJ: Princeton University Press.

Gragg, Charles I. 1940. "Because Wisdom Can't Be Told (HBSP Case 9- 451- 005)." Cambridge, MA: President and Fellows of Harvard College.

Gray, Paul S. 1980. "Exchange and Access in Field Work." *Urban Life* 9 (3): 309–31.

Greenhouse, Steven. 2020. "Will COVID-19 Spur a Wave of Unionization?" *Dissent* 67 (3): 112–14.

Guseva, Alya. 2020. *Into the Red: The Birth of the Credit Card Market in Postcommunist Russia*. Stanford, CA: Stanford University Press.

Hamann, Julian, and Stefan Beljean. 2021. "Career Gatekeeping in Cultural Fields." *American Journal of Cultural Sociology*, no. 9, 43–69.

Hanson, Rebecca, and Patricia Richards. 2019. *Harassed: Gender, Bodies, and Ethnographic Research*. Oakland: University of California Press.

Harrington, Brooke. 2003. "The Social Psychology of Access in Ethnographic Research." *Journal of Contemporary Ethnography* 32 (5): 592–625.

———. 2016. *Capital without Borders: Wealth Managers and the One Percent*. Cambridge, MA: Harvard University Press.

Harris, Leslie Maria, James T. Campbell, and Alfred L. Brophy. 2019. *Slavery and the University: Histories and Legacies*. Athens, GA: University of Georgia Press.

Hecht, Gabrielle. 1998. *The Radiance of France. Nuclear Power and National Identity after World War II*. Cambridge, MA: MIT Press.

Hirsch, Paul M. 1972. "Processing Fads and Fashions: An Organization-Set Analysis of Cultural Industry Systems." *American Journal of Sociology* 77 (4): 639–59.

Ho, Karen. 2009. *Liquidated: An Ethnography of Wall Street*. Durham, NC: Duke University Press.

Homans, George. 1993. *The Human Group*. New Brunswick, NJ: Transaction Publishers.

Hooker, Evelyn. 1993. "Reflections of a 40-Year Exploration: A Scientific View on Homosexuality." *American Psychologist* 48 (4): 450–53.

Hudson, Bryant A., and Gerardo A. Okhuysen. 2009. "Not with a Ten-Foot Pole: Core Stigma, Stigma Transfer, and Improbable Persistence of Men's Bath-houses." *Organization Science* 20 (1): 134–53.

Hughes, Everett C. 1974. "Who Studies Whom?" *Human Organization* 33 (4): 327–34.

Hunt, Linda. 1991. *Secret Agenda: The United States Government, Nazi Scientists, and Project Paperclip, 1945 to 1990*. New York: St. Martin's Press.

Iskander, Natasha. 2021. *Does Skill Make Us Human? Migrant Workers in 21st-Century Qatar and Beyond*. Princeton, NJ: Princeton University Press.

James-Enger, Kelly. 2013. *Goodbye Byline, Hello Big Bucks: Make Money Ghost-writing Books, Articles, Blogs, and More*. Downers Grove, IL: Improvise Press.

Jerolmack, Colin, and Alexandra K. Murphy. 2019. "The Ethical Dilemmas and Social Scientific Trade-Offs of Masking in Ethnography." *Sociological Methods & Research* 48 (4): 801–27.

Joy, Emile. 2014. *Freelance Writing Revealed: How to Make Money at Home by Ghostwriting and Freelance Writing*. CreateSpace.

Kahn, William A. 2015. *The Ostrich Effect: Solving Destructive Patterns at Work*. New York: Routledge.

Kalleberg, Arne L. 2011. *Good Jobs, Bad Jobs: The Rise of Polarized and Precarious Employment Systems in the United States, 1970s–2000s*. New York: Russell Sage Foundation.

Karabel, Jerome. 2005. *The Chosen: The Hidden History of Admission and Exclusion at Harvard, Yale, and Princeton*. Boston, MA: Houghton Mifflin Co.

Katz, Jack. 1982. *Poor People's Lawyers in Transition*. New Brunswick, NJ: Rutgers University Press.

———. 1988. *Seductions of Crime: Moral and Sensual Attractions in Doing Evil*. New York: Basic Books.

Keenan, Marie. 2013. *Child Sexual Abuse and the Catholic Church: Gender, Power, and Organizational Culture*. New York: Oxford University Press.

Kellogg, Katherine C. 2011. *Challenging Operations: Medical Reform and Resistance in Surgery*. Chicago, IL: University of Chicago Press.

Kempner, Joanna, Jon F. Merz, and Charles L. Bosk. 2011. "Forbidden Knowledge: Public Controversy and the Production of Nonknowledge." *Sociological Forum*, no. 26, 475–500.

Khurana, Rakesh. 2007. *From Higher Aims to Hired Hands: The Social Transformation of American Business Schools and the Unfulfilled Promise of Management as a Profession.* Princeton, NJ: Princeton University Press.

King, Brayden G., and Nicholas A. Pearce. 2010. "The Contentiousness of Markets: Politics, Social Movements, and Institutional Change in Markets." *Annual Review of Sociology*, no. 36, 249–67.

Kosatka, Art. 2011. "Recommended Security Guidelines for Airport Planning, Design and Construction." *Journal of Airport Management* 6 (1): 32–39.

Kunda, Gideon. 2009. *Engineering Culture: Control and Commitment in a High-Tech Corporation.* Philadelphia, PA: Temple University Press.

Lamont, Michèle. 2009. *How Professors Think: Inside the Curious World of Academic Judgment.* Cambridge, MA: Harvard University Press.

Lamont, Michèle, and Ann Swidler. 2014. "Methodological Pluralism and the Possibilities and Limits of Interviewing." *Qualitative Sociology* 37 (2): 153–71.

Lamouche, Robert. 1999. *Histoire du Centre Aéronautique de Melun-Villaroche: Melun-Villaroche, de 1936 à Nos Jours: Essais et Prototypes de l'Aviation Française.* Hericy, France: Éditions du Puits Fleuri.

Lareau, Annette. 2021. *Listening to People: A Practical Guide to Interviewing, Participant Observation, Data Analysis, and Writing It All Up.* Chicago, IL: University of Chicago Press.

Lindhout, Amanda, and Sara Corbett. 2013. *A House in the Sky: A Memoir.* New York: Scribner.

Locke, Karen, Karen Golden-Biddle, and Martha S. Feldman. 2008. "Making Doubt Generative: Rethinking the Role of Doubt in the Research Process." *Organization Science* 19 (6): 907–18.

Luker, Kristin. 2008. *Salsa Dancing into the Social Sciences.* Cambridge, MA: Harvard University Press.

Maitlis, Sally. 2011. "What Do You Care About? Studying What I Love." In *Research Alive: Exploring Generative Moments in Doing Qualitative Research*, edited by Arne Carlsen and Jane E. Dutton, 75–78. Liber: Copenhagen Business School Press.

Mazza, Ed. 2017. "'Art of the Deal' Co-author Tony Schwartz Predicts Trump's About to Resign." *Huffington Post*, August 17, 2017. https://www.huffpost.com/entry/tony-schwartz-trump-resign_n_59952d91e4b06ef724d64fd6.

McCormick, John. 2013. "Traveling Puppeteers." *World Encyclopedia of Puppetry Arts.* https://wepa.unima.org/en/travelling-puppeteers/.

McDonald, John. 2003. *A Ghost's Memoir: The Making of Alfred P. Sloan's* My Years with General Motors. Cambridge, MA: MIT Press.

McNamara, Robert P. 1994. *The Times Square Hustler: Male Prostitution in New York City.* Westport, CT: Praeger/Greenwood.

Meadow, Tey. 2013. "Studying Each Other: On Agency, Constraint, and Positionality in the Field." *Journal of Contemporary Ethnography* 42 (4): 466–81.

Michel, Alexandra. 2023. "Embodying the Market: The Emergence of the Body Entrepreneur." *Administrative Science Quarterly* 68 (1): 44–96.

Miller, Daniel. 2017. "Company Town: Disney Puppeteers Cry Foul over Show Closure." *The Los Angeles Times*, February 16, 2017.

Miller, Sally, and Cruz Santana. 2017. *Make Money as a Ghostwriter: How to Level Up Your Freelance Writing Business and Land Clients You Love*. Amazon.

Moffatt, Barton, and Carl Elliott. 2007. "Ghost Marketing: Pharmaceutical Companies and Ghostwritten Journal Articles." *Perspectives in Biology and Medicine* 50 (1): 18–31.

Morrill, Calvin. 1995. *The Executive Way: Conflict Management in Corporations*. Chicago, IL: University of Chicago Press.

Morrill, Calvin, Mayer N. Zald, and Hayagreeva Rao. 2003. "Covert Political Conflict in Organizations: Challenges from Below." *Annual Review of Sociology* 29 (1): 391–415.

Moskin, Julia. 2012. "I Was a Cookbook Ghostwriter." *New York Times*, March 14, 2012.

Murphey, Cecil. 2017. *Ghostwriting: The Murphey Method*. Phoenix, AZ: Christian Writers Institute.

Musselin, Christine. 2022. *La Longue Marche des Universités Françaises*. Paris: Presses de Sciences Po.

Naples, Nancy A. 1996. "A Feminist Revisiting of the Insider/Outsider Debate: The 'Outsider Phenomenon' in Rural Iowa." *Qualitative Sociology* 19 (1): 83–106.

Neely, Megan Tobias. 2022. *Hedged Out: Inequality and Insecurity on Wall Street*. Oakland, CA: University of California Press.

Noiriel, Gérard. 1990. "Journal de Terrain, Journal de Recherche et Auto-analyse. Entretien avec Florence Weber." *Genèses. Sciences Sociales et Histoire* 2 (1): 138–47.

Nouzille, Vincent. 1999. "La Folle Histoire du Dr Oestrich." LExpress.fr. May 20, 1999. //www.lexpress.fr/informations/la-folle-histoire-du-dr-oestrich_633746.html.

Olick, Jeffrey K., and Joyce Robbins. 1998. "Social Memory Studies: From 'Collective Memory' to the Historical Sociology of Mnemonic Practices." *Annual Review of Sociology* 24 (1): 105–40.

O'Mahony, Siobhán, and Fabrizio Ferraro. 2007. "The Emergence of Governance in an Open Source Community." *Academy of Management Journal* 50 (5): 1079–106.

Orta, Andrew. 2019. *Making Global MBAs: The Culture of Business and the Business of Culture*. Oakland, CA: University of California Press.

Padavic, Irene, Robin J. Ely, and Erin M. Reid. 2020. "Explaining the Persistence of Gender Inequality: The Work–Family Narrative as a Social Defense against the 24/7 Work Culture." *Administrative Science Quarterly* 65 (1): 61–111.

Parker, Ryan. 2017. "Jim Henson's Son Explains Why Kermit Actor Was Replaced." *The Hollywood Reporter*, July 18, 2017. http://www.nydailynews.com/entertainment/jim-henson-son-explains-kermit-actor-replaced-article-1.3336171.

Pascoe, C. J. 2007. *Dude, You're a Fag: Masculinity and Sexuality in High School.* Oakland, CA: University of California Press.

Pedicini, Sandra. 2016. "Disney World, Union Can't Agree: Are Festival of Fantasy 'Girls' Dancers or Performers?" *Orlando Sentinel.* September 7, 2016. https:// www.orlandosentinel.com/business/tourism/os-disney-world-dancer-parade -performer-pay-20160907-story.html.

Perlow, Leslie A. 2012. *Sleeping with Your Smartphone: How to Break the 24/7 Habit and Change the Way You Work.* Boston, MA: Harvard Business Review Press.

Petriglieri, Gianpiero, Susan J. Ashford, and Amy Wrzesniewski. 2019. "Agony and Ecstasy in the Gig Economy: Cultivating Holding Environments for Precarious and Personalized Work Identities." *Administrative Science Quarterly* 64 (1): 124–70.

Pfeffer, Jeffrey, and Gerald R. Salancik. 1978. *The External Control of Organizations: A Resource Dependence Perspective.* New York: Harper & Row.

Pugh, Allison J. 2009. *Longing and Belonging: Parents, Children, and Consumer Culture.* Berkeley, CA: University of California Press.

Rabinow, Paul. 1977. *Reflections on Fieldwork in Morocco.* Berkeley: University of California Press.

———. 2002. *French DNA: Trouble in Purgatory.* Chicago, IL: University of Chicago Press.

Rao, H., P. Monin, and R. Durand. 2003. "Institutional Change in Toque Ville: Nouvelle Cuisine as an Identity Movement in French Gastronomy." *American Journal of Sociology* 108 (4): 795–843.

Reilly, Patrick. 2018. "No Laughter among Thieves: Authenticity and the Enforcement of Community Norms in Stand-Up Comedy." *American Sociological Review* 83 (5): 933–58.

Ross, Joseph S., Kevin P. Hill, David S. Egilman, and Harlan M. Krumholz. 2008. "Guest Authorship and Ghostwriting in Publications Related to Rofecoxib: A Case Study of Industry Documents from Rofecoxib Litigation." *Journal of the American Medical Association* 299 (15): 1800–12.

Rothbard, Nancy P., and Lakshmi Ramarajan. 2009. "Checking Your Identities at the Door? Positive Relationships between Non-work and Work Identities." In *Exploring Positive Identities and Organizations: Building a Theoretical and Research Foundation,* edited by Laura Morgan Roberts and Jane Dutton, 125–48. New York: Psychology Press.

Rozsa, Matthew. 2017. "Workers at Disneyland Are Going Homeless." *Salon.* July 17, 2017. https://www.salon.com/2017/07/17/workers-disneyland-homeless/.

Rubin, Ashley T. 2021. *Rocking Qualitative Social Science: An Irreverent Guide to Rigorous Research.* Stanford, CA: Stanford University Press.

Sadler, Alfred M., Blair L. Sadler, and E. Blythe Stason. 1968. "The Uniform Anatomical Gift Act: A Model for Reform." *Journal of the American Medical Association* 206 (11): 2501–6.

Sallaz, Jeffrey J. 2009. *The Labor of Luck: Casino Capitalism in the United States and South Africa.* Berkeley, CA: University of California Press.

Sappol, Michael. 2002. *A Traffic of Dead Bodies: Anatomy and Embodied Social Identity in Nineteenth-Century America*. Princeton, NJ: Princeton University Press.

Scheper-Hughes, Nancy. 2001. *Saints, Scholars, and Schizophrenics: Mental Illness in Rural Ireland*. Berkeley, CA: University of California Press.

Schleef, Debra J. 2005. *Managing Elites: Socializaton in Law and Business Schools*. Oxford: Rowman & Littlefield.

Scott, James C. 1985. *Weapons of the Weak: Everyday Forms of Peasant Resistance*. New Haven, CT: Yale University Press.

Scranton, Philip. 2013. "Histories and Historical Ethnographies of Technical Practice: Managing Jet Propulsion in the US and France." *Entreprises et Histoire*, no. 4, 111–45.

Senior, Jennifer. 2020. "Happiness Won't Save You." *The New York Times*, November 24, 2020, sec. Opinion. https://www.nytimes.com/2020/11/24/opinion/happiness-depression-suicide-psychology.html.

Shaw, Eva. 2003. *Ghostwriting: For Fun & Profit*. Writeriffic Publishing Group.

———. 2012. *Ghostwriting: The Complete Guide*. Writeriffic Publishing Group.

Sheehan, Patrick. 2021. "Unemployment Experts: Governing the Job Search in the New Economy." *Work and Occupations* 48 (4): 470–97.

Sherman, Rachel. 2019. *Uneasy Street: The Anxieties of Affluence*. Princeton, NJ: Princeton University Press.

Shieber, Benjamin M. 1973. "Surface Bargaining: The Problem and a Proposed Solution." *University of Toledo Law Review*, no. 5, 656–80.

Simes, Jessica T., Bruce Western, and Angela Lee. 2022. "Mental Health Disparities in Solitary Confinement." *Criminology* 60 (3): 538–75.

Simmel, Georg. 1906. "The Sociology of Secrecy and of Secret Societies." *American Journal of Sociology* 11 (4): 441–98.

Small, Mario Luis, and Jessica McCrory Calarco. 2022. *Qualitative Literacy: A Guide to Evaluating Ethnographic and Interview Research*. Oakland, CA: University of California Press.

Smith, Carolyn D., and William Kornblum, eds. 1996. *In the Field: Readings on the Field Research Experience*. Westport, CT: Praeger.

Solans, Nerea Marteache. 2013. "Employee Theft from Passengers at US Airports: An Environmental Criminology Perspective." PhD diss., Rutgers University.

Stark, Alastair. 2020. "Left on the Shelf: Explaining the Failure of Public Inquiry Recommendations." *Public Administration* 98 (3): 609–24.

Stone, Amy L. 2018. "Queer Persistence in the Archive." In *Other, Please Specify: Queer Methods in Sociology*, edited by D'Lane R. Compton, Tey Meadow, and Kristen Schilt, 216–29. Oakland, CA: University of California Press.

Sweeney, Brigid. 2008. "Harvard Business School: Ain't No Party Like an HBS Party." *Boston Magazine*. https://www.bostonmagazine.com/2008/08/19/aint-no-party-like-an-hbs-party/.

Taussig, Michael. 2010. *Walter Benjamin's Grave*. Chicago, IL: University of Chicago Press.

Tilcsik, András, Michel Anteby, and Carly R Knight. 2015. "Concealable Stigma and Occupational Segregation: Toward a Theory of Gay and Lesbian Occupations." *Administrative Science Quarterly* 60 (2): 446–81.

Timmermans, Stefan. 2007. *Postmortem: How Medical Examiners Explain Suspicious Deaths*. Chicago, IL: University of Chicago Press.

Timmermans, Stefan, and Iddo Tavory. 2012. "Theory Construction in Qualitative Research: From Grounded Theory to Abductive Analysis." *Sociological Theory* 30 (3): 167–86.

———. 2022. *Data Analysis in Qualitative Research: Theorizing with Abductive Analysis*. Chicago, IL: University of Chicago Press.

Toubiana, Madeline, and Trish Ruebottom. 2022. "Stigma Hierarchies: The Internal Dynamics of Stigmatization in the Sex Work Occupation." *Administrative Science Quarterly* 67 (2): 515–52.

Trump, Donald. 1987. *Trump: The Art of the Deal*. New York: Random House.

Turco, Catherine J. 2016. *The Conversational Firm: Rethinking Bureaucracy in the Age of Social Media*. New York: Columbia University Press.

US Government Accountability Office. 2012. "Air Passenger Screening: Transportation Security Administration Could Improve Complaint Processes." GAO-13-4. Washington, DC: US Government Accountability Office.

———. 2013. "Transportation Security Administration Could Strengthen Monitoring of Allegations." Report GAO-13-624. Washington, DC: US Government Accountability Office.

Van Maanen, John. 1973. "Observations on the Making of Policemen." *Human Organization* 32 (4): 407–18.

———. 1983. "Golden Passports: Managerial Socialization and Graduate Education." *The Review of Higher Education* 6 (4): 435–55.

———. 1991. "The Smile Factory." In *Reframing Organizational Culture*, edited by Peter J. Frost, Larry F. Moore, Meryl Reis Louis, Craig C. Lundberg, and Joanne Martin, 58–76. Newbury Park, CA: Sage Publications.

———. 2011. *Tales of the Field: On Writing Ethnography*. Chicago, IL: University of Chicago Press.

———. 2020. "Withdrawal Pains and Gains: Exiting from the Field." In *The Routledge Companion to Anthropology and Business*, edited by Raza Mir and Anne-Laure Fayard, 501–13. New York: Routledge.

Van Maanen, John, and Deborah Kolb. 1985. "The Professional Apprentice: Observations on Fieldwork Roles in Two Organizational Settings." In *Research in the Sociology of Organizations*, edited by S. B. Bacharach and S. M. Mitchell, 4:1–33. Greenwich, CT: JAI Press.

Vaughan, Diane. 1996. *The Challenger Launch Decision: Risky Technology, Culture, and Deviance at NASA*. Chicago, IL: University of Chicago Press.

———. 2002. "Signals and Interpretive Work: The Role of Culture in a Theory of Practical Action." In *Culture in Mind: Toward a Sociology of Culture and Cognition*, edited by Karen A. Cerulo, 28–54. New York: Routledge.

———. 2021. *Dead Reckoning: Air Traffic Control, System Effects, and Risk*. Chicago, IL: University of Chicago Press.

Venkatesh, Sudhir. 2013. "Underground Markets as Fields in Transition: Sex Work in New York City." In *Sociological Forum*, no. 28, 682–99.

Verdery, Katherine. 2018. *My Life as a Spy: Investigations in a Secret Police File.* Durham, NC: Duke University Press.

Vertesi, Janet. 2015. *Seeing Like a Rover: How Robots, Teams, and Images Craft Knowledge of Mars.* Chicago, IL: University of Chicago Press.

Wacquant, Loïc. 2004. *Body & Soul: Ethnographic Notebooks of an Apprentice Boxer.* New York: Oxford University Press.

———. 2005. "Carnal Connections: On Embodiment, Apprenticeship, and Membership." *Qualitative Sociology* 28 (4): 445–74.

Ward, Jane. 2018. "The Methods Gatekeepers and the Exiled Queers." In *Other, Please Specify: Queer Methods in Sociology*, edited by D'Lane R. Compton, Tey Meadow, and Kristen Schilt, 51–66. Oakland, CA: University of California Press.

Warikoo, Natasha K. 2016. *The Diversity Bargain and Other Dilemmas of Race, Admissions, and Meritocracy at Elite Universities.* Chicago, IL: University of Chicago Press.

Weil, David. 2014. *The Fissured Workplace.* Cambridge, MA: Harvard University Press.

Whitworth, Laura. 2015. *Ghostwriter's 101: How to Get into Ghostwriting and Make It a Business.* Amazon.

Whyte, William Foote. 1993. *Street Corner Society: The Social Structure of an Italian Slum.* 4th ed. Chicago, IL: University of Chicago Press.

Williams, Terry. 1996. "Exploring the Cocaine Culture." In *In the Field: Readings on the Field Research Experience*, edited by Carolyn D. Smith and William Kornblum, 27–32. Westport, CT: Praeger/Greenwood.

Winter, Jay. 2010. "Thinking about Silence." In *Shadows of War: A Social History of Silence in the Twentieth Century*, edited by Efrat Ben-Ze'ev, Ruth Ginio, and Jay Winter, 3–31. Cambridge, UK: Cambridge University Press.

Zaloom, Caitlin. 2019. *Indebted: How Families Make College Work at Any Cost.* Princeton, NJ: Princeton University Press.

Zbaracki, Mark J., and Mark Bergen. 2010. "When Truces Collapse: A Longitudinal Study of Price-Adjustment Routines." *Organization Science* 21 (5): 955–72.

Zelizer, Viviana. 2005. "Circuits within Capitalism." In *The Economic Sociology of Capitalism*, edited by Victor Nee and Richard Swedberg, 289–322. Princeton, NJ: Princeton University Press.

Zerubavel, Eviatar. 2006. *The Elephant in the Room: Silence and Denial in Everyday Life.* Oxford University Press.

———. 2010. "The Social Sound of Silence: Toward a Sociology of Denial." In *Shadows of War: A Social History of Silence in the Twentieth Century*, edited by Efrat Ben-Ze'ev, Ruth Ginio, and Jay Winter, 32–44. Cambridge, UK: Cambridge University Press.

INDEX

Page numbers followed by an 'n' indicate notes.

A NOTE ON THE TYPE

THIS BOOK has been composed in Miller, a Scotch Roman typeface designed by Matthew Carter and first released by Font Bureau in 1997. It resembles Monticello, the typeface developed for The Papers of Thomas Jefferson in the 1940s by C. H. Griffith and P. J. Conkwright and reinterpreted in digital form by Carter in 2003.

Pleasant Jefferson ("P. J.") Conkwright (1905–1986) was Typographer at Princeton University Press from 1939 to 1970. He was an acclaimed book designer and AIGA Medalist.

GPSR Authorized Representative: Easy Access System Europe - Mustamäe tee
50, 10621 Tallinn, Estonia, gpsr.requests@easproject.com